To Jo

with best wishes
and thanks for
looking after
our garden!

13. 3. 06.

Carl F Flesch was born in 1910 and spent his formative years in Germany. Having had to give up his legal career owing to the advent of the Nazis, he emigrated to London where he became an insurance broker specialising in insurance for musicians and contingency covers. Subsequently he became - for his sins, as he says, a "name" at Lloyd's.

He discovered his talent for writing only after retirement; this is his fourth book. He lives in London and his main interests are music, reading and Bridge; as he is the first to admit, he firmly belongs in the category of "kitchen bridge players".

WHO'S NOT WHO
AND OTHER MATTERS

Carl F Flesch

Who's Not Who
And Other Matters

Vanguard Press

A CIP catalogue record for this title is
available from the British Library

ISBN 1 84386 244 1

*Vanguard Press is an imprint of
Pegasus Elliot MacKenzie Publishers Ltd.*
www.pegasuspublishers.com

First Published in 2006

**Vanguard Press
Sheraton House Castle Park
Cambridge England**

Printed & Bound in Great Britain

"To my wives, Ruth and Sheila, and my daughter, Carol, in loving memory"

Books published by Carl F Flesch

"And do you also play the violin?", Toccata Press, 1990
German edition: "Und spielts Du auche Geie?" Schott
Soehne, 1990

"Inside Insurance", Management 2000 Ltd., 1998
German edition: Makler werden ist nicht schwer,…Verlag
Versicherungswirtschft, Karlsruhe, 1996

"Where do you come from?" Pen Press, 2001
German edition: "Woher kmmen Sie?" Verlag Rdinhold
Kraemer, Hamburg, 2003

Contents

Introduction

Who you are or what you are?

*"What's wrong with being a boring
kind of guy?"*

George W. Bush,
American President

Who is regarded as the greater hero? The Olympic gold
medallist cheered by the crowd, or the soldier in battle
putting his life at risk every day, but who is "only" in the
constant thoughts of his family? No prizes are offered for the
answer[1].

But this misjudgement does not apply only to heroes: it
is the accepted wisdom that for a biography, auto-biography
or similar book to appeal to a wider audience, it has to be by
or about a person in one of two categories. In the first, the
subject may be a fairly average person who, however, has a
specifically intriguing tale to tell, such as, for instance, a
former explorer, spy, holocaust survivor, rescued kidnap
victim or even a criminal, convicted or acquitted, reformed or
unreformed. The list, incidentally, also extends to
occupations that at first glance appear to be more
commonplace, such as doctors, lawyers, and, curiously
enough, taxi drivers (I remember several quite successful
memoirs in this latter field). The reason is probably that these
books give the reader the illusion of eavesdropping on others
in unguarded situations or moments.

In the second category the author has to be a famous

---

[1] This is the theme of the book "Heroes, Saviours, Traitors and
Supermen by Lucy Hughes-Hallet – Fourth Estate 2004)

person, be it an actor, musician, politician, painter, writer, model or footballer (at least as long as he does not miss vital penalties; if on the other hand he is addicted to drink or drugs, he remains thoroughly newsworthy). Yet, take away the fame, and you will find that what remains in many instances is no more interesting (and sometimes less – *vide* the implied admission by George Bush) than the lives, and thoughts of average persons with their individual experiences, ideas, successes, failures and conscious or subconscious urges and motivations. But the biographies and thoughts of these "normal" unremarkable individuals won't grip the imagination of the public. The reader does not really want to know about people who are, at least at first glance, no different from the great masses. I maintain that, for this reason, he or she may be missing quite a lot that is very worthwhile.

This is not difficult to illustrate. Take Arthur Miller's "Time Bends", a fascinating bestseller. Yet is what he describes, for instance his childhood, in any way different from that of most ordinary boys? Disliking certain foods, giggling in class, releasing fire flies, falling off a bike, disagreements with parents, even intending or trying to run away from home – who hasn't had similar experiences? In Arthur Miller's case they were not in any way more remarkable at the time than those of other children. They became so only when in later life he developed into a world-famous playwright. But why should they, for that reason, suddenly have changed their character and become more interesting than before? Of course, he describes them in an unmatched style, but this is just the point I want to make: if he had done this in precisely the same way as John Smith without the fame attached to his name, probably nobody would have bothered to buy the book (if he had managed to find anyone to publish it in the first place) and the world would have been deprived of something very readable..

Or take the almost opposite case – a recent biography of P. G. Wodehouse. Quite a few reviewers lauded the book mainly because the author had managed to write so interestingly on the basis of comparatively scanty material. For whilst Wodehouse was a comic writer of genius, he was, by all accounts, not a very remarkable person and his life was comparatively uneventful; apart, that is, from the one well-known discreditable episode, his broadcasts from Germany during World War II, which showed him up as outstandingly naïve and inept. We read the biography not because it describes an interesting life, but for no other reason than that it is about a famous person, whose works speak much better for him than any biography could. There are non-famous lives whose description would be much more rewarding.

All this is undoubtedly true until we come to fiction. Here, curiously enough, almost the opposite applies. In the majority of cases, we don't object at all to reading about ordinary people, and even like to identify with them. And the subject matter does not always have to be intriguing either: the brothers Grossmith's "Diary of a Nobody" was in its time a bestseller and remains a classic. What could be more humdrum than the events described in that book – and yet at the same time so fascinating to the reader?

Why should this be valid only for fiction? Why should events and ideas in the life of an ordinary person be less interesting than those of imaginary or sometimes real-life famous ones? Well, I believe the simple answer is that they aren't, if only because no-one is really "ordinary". To turn, if I may, to my own case, I regard myself as an average person. My achievements, such as they are, cannot be called spectacular. Yet I nevertheless believe that parts of my experiences and ideas are no less noteworthy than those of the "average celebrity" if I may be allowed to use this somewhat contradictory term.

In this book I have tried to put this to the test. The sections that follow are partly semi-autobiographical, partly on general topics and partly on matters on which I expressed thoughts, which sometimes aroused rather uncomplimentary reactions. But nobody has as yet called them boring, at least not to my face.

Moreover, I have noticed that, whilst people who criticise my views may well be right, they rarely produce really convincing counter arguments of their own. I dare not express the expectation that this means I shall be proved right one day, for I have to admit that I do not have a very good track record where predictions are concerned: when I saw "The Mousetrap" (as I write this, in its 50th year) about 6 weeks after its first performance, I confidently declared: this one is going to fold shortly. 30 years on, a theatre producer of my acquaintance, considering to take the play in translation to Germany, asked me to get him tickets for it. I decided to tag along, since it seemed obvious that I had made a slight miscalculation at the time, and I wanted to know the reason why. When we emerged from the theatre after the performance, I was moved to exclaim: I *still* do not believe that this play can run for long. Obviously, I can't help it, or at least my predictions take a very long time to come true, which, I have to admit, must be regarded as somewhat self-contradictory in the case of the "Mousetrap".

This book occasionally contains topics on which I have touched previously in different contexts; sometimes they are simple reprints, sometimes I have rewritten them. One such piece, "Class and the subconscious mind, any connection", appeared, under a different title, in "Mensa Magazine" a great many years ago and engendered a lively, mainly critical, even hostile, correspondence. I recall one member calling me "stupid", surely a unique expression of opinion by one Mensan about another. On the other hand, as a psychologist once told me, the IQ of the average grammar school boy is quite sufficient to qualify him for Mensa; and, after all, there are bound to be stupid grammar school boys.

I have never understood why anyone should get hot under the collar when disagreeing even on cherished beliefs. Controversy, as they say, inevitably sharpens the mind and keeps the adrenalin flowing. I have known a number of people – the famous pianist Artur Schnabel was a foremost example – who, in company, took a particular delight in always taking the opposite position to any opinion that happened to be expressed. I don't hold with that, of course, yet, to coin a phrase, how boring life would be if we all held the same views!

Thus I hope to demonstrate that a work of non-fiction by a non-famous person can be a good read, and I win either way: no matter whether people buy this book and like it or whether they don't buy it or don't like it, I shall have proved my point. Whether my publishers will be happy with the second possibility, is another matter.

Interlude

Meaningless wisdom?

And that's only what they said
before breakfast

In my foreword I set out as one of my aims to show that some little-known people may be just as interesting and profound as famous ones. If I may, I'll go a step further; I find not infrequently that pearls of wisdom from the prominent can be quite meaningless. It is not that I disagree with them, to me they simply do not make sense.

I realise that I am sticking my neck out and exposing myself to the risk of considerable ridicule in case I have misjudged these sayings…Am I just too stupid or uneducated to understand and appreciate them? In some cases this may be true, but surely – hopefully – not in all of them. Let you, my readers, be the judges.

I have taken, almost at random, 12 such sayings from a dictionary of quotations. The compilers of these works have my sympathy; it is their job to fill a certain number of pages in order to make the book commercially viable. It is not their job to judge whether the sayings they quote are "good" or "bad" – and they don't. All that matters to them is that they have been uttered by prominent people and are therefore "quotable". This, of course, is where we came in.

*The present is the ever-moving shadow that divides yesterday
from today. In this lies hope.*

Frank Lloyd Wrigh.t

Why on earth should this cause us to hope, and hope what?

Men who work cannot dream and wisdom comes to us only in dreams.

Prophet Snohalla.

Work and dreams are, of course, not mutually exclusive, and wisdom certainly does not come in dreams. But what a convenient excuse for spending your life doing nothing!

Age does not matter unless you are a cheese.

Billie Burke.

This is actually the title of a compilation of quotations and it is, I admit, quite eye-catching. But clearly, Mr Burke has never eaten fish or meat that has gone off, or broke a tooth on a 6 months' old biscuit.

What is called Youth is not youth, it is rather something like premature old age.

Henry Miller.

I wonder how old Henry Miller was when he said that.

A little money helps, but what really gets it right is never – I repeat never – to face the facts.

Ruth Gordon.

Well, some books on self-improvement are equally silly, and at least we didn't have to pay for this one.

> *The most precious gift – Doubt.*
>
> *Jorge Louis Borges.*

Well, I rather doubt that...

> *Any life, no matter how long and complex it may be, is made up of a single moment – the moment in which a man finds out once and for all, who he is.*
>
> *Jorge Louis Borges.*

Explain!

> *It is the beginning of the end when you discover you have style.*
>
> *Dashiell Hammett.*

Boy, am I glad not to have discovered it yet!

> *Hope resides in the meaning of what our lives have been.*
>
> *S.B. Nuland.*

Eh?

> *It is better to be approximately right than precisely wrong.*
>
> *Warren Buffet.*

Too true! And it is better to be rich, young and healthy rather than poor, old and sick.

I do not believe that optimism can come about except through true tragedy.

Madeleine l'Engle.

You could have fooled me!

The only sin is mediocrity.

Martha Graham.

At last we know the reason why so few people make it to heaven.

Well, how was it for you?

1

Briefly

"The reader need not become uneasy;
I do not intend to write of the Boy who made good"

Neville Cardus

I suppose I'd better start with summarising the events of my life, such as they are. This won't take long, as some are referred to in various sections that follow and others in books I have written previously[2]. There is thus no need to repeat them here at any length.

I was born on June 23, 1910, in Rindbach, Austria, a village not far from the famous White Horse Inn, where my parents for some years regularly spent their summer holidays in the company of friends. At that time, childbirths were taken more in their stride than they are today and my parents evidently found nothing wrong with entrusting the handling of the whole affair to the local village doctor. All went well, although I turned out to be one of a pair of twins, something that was not predictable at the time.

Neither I nor any other member of my family have a drop of *non*-Jewish blood in us, but my father found it politic to have us children baptised (my brother and me at the tender age of 14 days), since, at that time, it was an established fact that in Germany people of Christian faith had far better career chances than Jews; before the Nazis this was almost entirely a question of adherence to the Christian religion and not one of race. Much as I now regret my parents' decision, I appreciate that they took it in the best interests of my siblings and myself, as they saw them at the time. My father had no need

---

[2] Mainly my books "and do you also play the violin?" and "Where do you come from?"

to worry about this question for himself: he was an internationally famous violinist, for whom the adherence to whatever religion he chose did not matter. In fact, at the beginning of the century he had, for about 5 years, been "court violinist" to the Queen of Romania, a country whose main characteristic was notoriously not a love of Jews.

Whilst at school I participated in Christian religious instruction, religion itself played no part whatever in my parents' house and did not constitute any problem. Subsequently, when race became the only relevant criterion, I left the Christian Church, which in Germany could be done by simple declaration.

At that time we lived in Berlin, where I went to school until, at 15, I was sent to a boarding school. I had been, for reasons, on which I am speculating in a later section, a very bad pupil. My transfer to the famous "Salem" boarding school, was made partly in order to try and remedy this, and partly to make sure that I was being looked after properly whilst my parents regularly spent five months of the year in USA, where my father was head of the violin department at the newly founded Curtis Institute of Music in Philadelphia. Again, the boarding school and its effect on me are described later in this book, so I need not dwell on them here.

After completing my A levels, I studied law at the universities of Freiburg, Heidelberg, and mainly Berlin and passed my university final examination in 1931. At that time, these finals were very strict indeed, culminating in a well-attended public oral examination. If you did not pass, you were never told in what subject you had failed, so that you had to do the whole thing again, which took about 6 months. You were allowed only two attempts, unless you got special dispensation from the Department of Justice for a third try. Thus it was a very stressful procedure. Whether it produced better lawyers than in other countries is another question.

After completing university studies, every German budding lawyer has to become a *Referendar,* an unpaid civil servant, in order to acquire practical experience in all branches of legal administration. This takes three years. Originally my family were Hungarian nationals, which would have made it impossible for me to become a civil servant. I had therefore to acquire German nationality and since I was still under age, the whole family became naturalised Germans. This was a few years prior to Hitler's accession to power and shows how impossible it was at the time to imagine the developments that followed. At my final examination, though my marks had only been average, I had been complimented by the head of the examining board on having got through my university studies so speedily and at so young an age, a fact of which I was very proud. Possibly if I had completed my training at a somewhat slower pace and therefore reached the age of majority, I would have spared my family a lot of trouble later: they would not, like me, have had to become Germans.

When, in January 1933, the Nazis came to power, Jewish civil servants were, of course, the first to be dismissed and there was no possibility of continuing in my chosen career. In spite of my belonging to the Christian Church, I had never made a secret of my being of Jewish descent and was rightly of course, regarded by the authorities as a Jew.

I emigrated from Germany in August 1933, thus avoiding the horrors of the later Nazi years, yet my departure was pretty traumatic all the same. After a six months' stay in Holland, my mother's country of birth, I decided to move to England.

Un-typically, I was able to enter the country without any difficulty: my father had an engagement with the BBC for a sonata recital with the pianist (and Beethoven look-a-like) Frederick Lamond, and simply took me along as his "secretary". Thereafter, my time-limited residence permit was always renewed without trouble. This, of course, did not extend to any permission to accept work, paid or unpaid. I have described the ins and outs of this problem elsewhere.

I was resolved not to study law again. There was, at that time, no certainty that any German refugee would be permitted to stay in Great Britain permanently, and I did not care to risk studying for a second time a subject that could be of use only in the country of one's residence. One set of five wasted years seemed to me quite ample.

I decided to become an insurance broker, mistakenly believing that this profession had something to do with the Law. I obtained a work permit at my second attempt and, starting from scratch, managed, in partnership with a more experienced colleague, like me a refugee, to establish a small business. With a tiny income, I married a lovely girl, Ruth, who most unfortunately, after the birth of our second child developed occasional episodes of post-natal depression, which continued to plague her for the rest of her life and would materialise at the most unexpected times. In the 1940s, medical science was even less able to cope effectively with this illness than today. One curious but unmistakable side effect of this relative lack of knowledge was that doctors carrying out the treatment, such as it was, often nurtured some usually quite unfounded hostility towards the spouses of their patients, which did not make matters any easier. It would be wrong to say that this complaint did not affect our life style, for one thing it was difficult to make plans in advance, but it made absolutely no difference to the solidity of our marriage. Ruth was outstandingly attractive both in looks and by character and beloved by all who knew her. Tragically, she died at the age of 70 from an illness not connected with her previous complaint in any way.

At the beginning of World War II, I was not yet naturalised British and my application to join the army as a volunteer was refused due to my former German nationality; "former", because I had, like every emigrant German Jew, been deprived by the Nazis of my German citizenship. However, my father being Hungarian by birth, I had automatically acquired that nationality, too. To my agreeable surprise I ascertained that I had not in fact lost it through my subsequent German naturalisation. For this reason we were fortunate enough to spend the first war years (until Hungary entered the war on Germany's side) as "friendly (as opposed to 'enemy') aliens." In this way I escaped the internment of most refugees after the collapse of France, when practically every person coming from Germany was regarded as a potential fifth columnist and treated accordingly, an outstandingly futile and hurtful measure as far as we refugees were concerned.

For about 18 months I did voluntary war work in factories in very lowly positions, but then returned to my original business a "reserved occupation" as it happened. After the war, my firm became reasonably prosperous, though I would not call it hugely successful, until I allowed myself to be persuaded to amalgamate with another, much larger and longer-established company and go public, something which was much easier then than it is today. This turned out to be one of the most serious mistakes I ever made in my life. For many reasons, small firms should not become publicly quoted companies. Moreover, unbeknown to me (and my professional advisers, whom nowadays I would probably have been able to sue for negligence – a possibility nobody thought of at the time), the other firm's business had, when we amalgamated, already been seriously flawed and after a few years matters began to go badly wrong. My radical plans designed to save the situation were not accepted by my colleagues on the board, and I resigned. The sale of my shares, resulting in an amount which by today's standards would be quite risible, would at that time have been sufficient for me to retire in comparative comfort and bring up my two children. This was, in fact, a definite option inasmuch as, due to a non-competition agreement, whose introduction had originally been *my* suggestion, I was not permitted to work as an insurance broker for two years. However, in my mid-fifties, retirement was unthinkable to me.

Foolishly, I did not do what I should have done – grasp the opportunity to recommence my law studies, which would still have been a possibility, but rather marked time. After two years I took up my insurance career again in association with others, on the way becoming an underwriting member of Lloyd's, my second big mistake. Unfortunately my broking partners and I were not at all compatible and trading results were highly unsatisfactory. Again, I resigned, but not wishing to conclude my career on so unsatisfactory a note even though pushing 70, I wrote to the 12 largest Lloyd's brokers in the country, offering my services in building up a German connection. It would, of course, have been the height of folly to mention my age in my letters of application, so I simply wrote that I had "decades of experience". I got away with it, 6 interviews and 2 job offers, though it sometimes needed a thick skin when observing the reaction of potential employers as they got to see me in person.

I accepted the job offer that suited me best, my first time as an employee at the age of 70, and I spent eight highly satisfactory and not unsuccessful years with the largest broking firm in the country. Being as it were at the other end of the scale: compared to my own previous firms, I realised how much easier, let alone more profitable, it is to concentrate on big rather than on small business. At the age of 78, I did retire.

However, I am an unrepentant workaholic and could not bear sitting back and doing nothing. I became an occasional consultant to a Lloyd's syndicate, wrote three books, which were published both in English and German, and in addition became London correspondent for a prominent German insurance journal, reporting fortnightly on the British insurance scene, a position from which I resigned after twelve years. And, though well into my nineties, I still miss work and in particular, writing. Whether this justifies yet another book, I have to leave to my readers to judge.

2

Who's not Who

"Hello, I am Julian and this is my friend Sandy."

Catchphrase from BBC serial
"Around the Horne"

A good point to start is the long-running BBC radio programme "Desert Island Discs", in which interviews of prominent people are interspersed with the playing of a few snatches from the eight records they would most wish to have with them if they were to be marooned on a desert island. Not infrequently, the items selected are musically decidedly unremarkable, but are supposed to be a pointer to the make-up and character of the person interviewed. At least that is the theory. I can't prove it, of course, but I have the distinct feeling that in many cases the interviewee could not care less. And I am not the only one in suspecting this: I remember a comedy (whose title I have forgotten) in which a famous actor is to appear on "Desert Island Discs" in 3 days' time; and is still desperately casting around for the pieces of music indispensable for his well-being and happiness in his lonely exile. To some if not most people appearing on that programme, the music does not seem to matter[3]; it is the accolade of being asked to be part of it that does.

In spite of the musical name, the main attraction for most of the audience is not the choice of music either, but the

---

[3] Nor, apparently, overmuch to the BBC. I remember a friend of mine for whom I went to some trouble to confirm the title of one of the pieces he was anxious to have played, having to drop it;. the programmers considered that it did not "fit in."

prominent position of the person choosing it. The instinctive belief is that, if a person has achieved fame in one particular field, everything else about him or her must also be special and interesting. The same or better choice of records by an unknown Mr. X or Miss Y would not grab their attention, however interesting their story or original and profound their ideas might be. As I said in my introduction, if you are not famous, there is no real impact. Yet it is an undeniable fact that, with exceptions of course, talent in one particular field does not necessarily make you interesting in other respects; and the opposite is true as well. This is remarkable for a reason to which I have also referred in my foreword: fictional heroes or heroines do not have to be outstanding at all to make a successful novel. Yes, you will say, it is the way their story is being told that is gripping. Precisely the point I am trying to make: there are a lot of interesting or amusing things to say about people who can make no claim to real fame, "it's the way you tell them".

As the son of an internationally renowned musician, I have, in my parents' house, probably met more famous personalities than my fair share. Admittedly I was young and not very observant. But by and large, as far as I could see, their outstanding talent in one respect did not make them more remarkable in others. Conversation, of course, was frequently shoptalk and over my head. But otherwise it amounted to surprisingly little. The conversations of ordinary people were often far more rewarding.

Allow me to try and prove my point. Let us look at a few men and women I have known who undoubtedly achieved quite a lot in their chosen field, but none of whom can be called really "famous" in the sense that their biography or memoirs would have attracted the attention of more than a fraction of those who would have avidly read a book about, shall we say, a pop artist with nothing but a few ephemeral best-selling singles to his credit. Let us see whether there are not at least a few titbits and anecdotes (no more) about them just as amusing as those about popular icons.

I first met *Peter Diamand* in Berlin, where we were both students. When after Hitler's rise to power he was, like me, no longer able to follow his chosen career he became PA to the pianist, Artur Schnabel, in which capacity he gained a thorough knowledge of music, concert life and everything that makes musicians tick. When Schnabel moved to the United States, Peter went to Holland where, in 1940, he was trapped by the German invasion. He was able to escape from a concentration camp and survived the war in hiding, where he passed the time putting together plans for a Music Festival. When after the war the "Holland Festival" was born with him as managing director, it soon became one of the leading annual musical events in Europe. Subsequently he was headhunted for the directorship of the Edinburgh Festival as successor to the Queen's cousin Lord Harewood and managed it very successfully until he reached retirement age. Thereafter he became artistic adviser to one of the leading French symphony orchestras as well as casting director for some of the opera CDs conducted by Daniel Barenboim.

Nobody could call him good-looking, yet his charm, wit and personality made him highly attractive to everybody he met, not least to women. No lesser Goddess – and this may well be the most interesting thing about him, as far as the general public is concerned – than Marlene Dietrich hints in one of her numerous autobiographies at a brief affair with him, identifying him by his initials and describing him as "a little Jew". His reaction was, "I am little and I am a Jew, but for the rest, no comment." After his death the veracity of the story was confirmed to me by an impeccable source, How many people, famous or not, can boast (or, in his case, not boast) of a similar success in their love life?

During his first years as a director at Edinburgh he lived, and fathered a child, with a well-known musician who subsequently became his second wife. But before this marriage, the true facts had, to the amusement of those in the know, to be kept strictly hidden from the, at that time, still highly puritanical Edinburgh city fathers, quite a remarkable feat in itself.

He was a most amusing raconteur. I have retold one of his stories in number 12 "Enigmas". I tried repeatedly to motivate him to write his memoirs, but he always refused, probably sensing that they would not be recognised for their real worth. However, he recorded in France a series of broadcasts about famous musicians he had met, sprinkling them (the broadcasts, not the musicians!) with examples of their art. The BBC could not be induced to broadcast them with English voiceovers, which would have been easy enough, a remarkable illustration of the fact that programme makers themselves are not free from the "famous name syndrome". One day, who knows, they may think better of it.

Probably the most talented pupil my father ever had was the child prodigy *Josef Hassid*. Of him, no lesser person than Fritz Kreisler, said, after he had heard him in one of my father's lessons: "A Menuhin is born every 100 years, a Hassid every 200 years." Unfortunately, he developed schizophrenia at a very early age and did not survive a leucotomy operation. The reason why he is so little remembered is that, in his short career, he had time to make only one record with a few short pieces, issued by HMV under the title "The complete Hassid". They are sufficient to show what the world has missed by his early death.

Whilst in compulsory confinement in a mental institution, he was said to have made a blacklist naming the people he would murder, were he ever to get free. At the top of this list was *Harold Holt*, the head of the, at that time, indisputably leading British concert agency bearing his name. The black joke among professional musicians, not known for their love of concert agents, was: "Hassid can't be all that mad if he wants to kill Harold Holt". An unfair remark: Holt was undoubtedly a sharp businessman, but equally without question perfectly straight. His story, often retold by him, of Richard Tauber cancelling an Albert Hall matinee half-an-hour before its start, because "he could not give of his best", will be for ever in my memory. Holt had had to return the ticket monies for a sold-out Albert Hall and I believe, never got quite over the trauma of it.[4] I did some business with his firm and remember a nice turn of phrase, with which he refused one of my propositions: "Flesch is willing, but we are not".

Talking of concert agents and promoters, they are, as I said, members of a much-maligned profession. Artists, unless they are at the very top of the tree, tend to complain that the agent is not getting them a sufficient number of engagements, and then not at the fee they deserve. This is rarely true. The competition between first-class artists is immense and there is only a limited number of concerts featuring classical music. In my profession as an insurance broker, I worked with many such agents and found them, with few exceptions, doing a very capable job.

One of them was, or rather is, I am glad to say, *Victor Hochhauser.* He has promoted appearances by world famous Russian artists such as David Oistrakh, Rostropovitch, Richter (a particular gamble, for Richter was apt to cancel at the shortest of notices and fairly regularly at that) and Nureyev. He brought the Bolshoi and the Kyrov companies to London, both for opera and ballet. But perhaps his most remarkable feat was the promotion of regular popular classical symphony concerts with good financial success, thereby hitting the theory on the head that good music has always to be subsidised. He managed this by engaging good orchestras, conductors and soloists who were, however, not top names asking for fees that make practically any concert in which they appear, commercially non-viable without a sponsor. Were his concerts then, as one might suppose at first glance, some of the few instances in which the "famous name syndrome" has no validity? I don't think so: the famous

---

[4] Insuring Tauber's concerts against cancellation became impossible as a result. But this was, in fact, doing him an injustice. I happened to know him quite well and had numerous examples testifying to his being a real trouper. For him, not being able to give of his best was not an excuse, but a genuine reason for cancelling a concert.

names were the composers; without them the halls would have been empty.

He has a ready wit. At the time of the Irish terror acts, I once suggested to him an insurance against the risk of having to vacate the Albert Hall due to a bomb threat and having to return all the ticket monies. "My dear chap", he replied, "the only bomb threat I am concerned with is the risk of the canons in Tschaikowky's 1812 overture not going off." He is also able to cope superbly with the unexpected; he was probably the only promoter whose scheduled concert went ahead on the day King George V died and public mourning was decreed, cancelling any public event. He had arranged a concert by the Vienna Boys Choir and saved it by changing the programme to religious songs only. The story that the audience demanded the "Blue Danube" as an encore is, one must hope, nothing but an ugly rumour.

Another agent I particularly liked was *Sandor Gorlinsky*. He had started on one of the lowest rungs of the ladder, as a redcoat at a Butlins holiday camp, but through his own efforts became the impresario and agent who, after World War II, brought La Scala of Milan to England and represented artists of the calibre of Giulini, Gobbi, Toscanini, Tebaldi, Nureyev, Makarova, Raimondo, Caballé, Carreras and a host of others. Last but not least he introduced Maria Callas to British audiences. After her divorce from Meneghini, who had handled all her business affairs, she unhesitatingly appointed Gorlinsky as her personal manager and stayed with him throughout the remainder of her professional career. You cannot build up such a clientele unless you are exceptional both in character and in achievements. In his special field of representing singers, his leadership was undisputed. He told me once that he no longer had to approach opera houses to ask whether they might be prepared to engage one of his artists. All he had to say was something like "I can let you have so-and-so for such and such dates" and they would usually jump at it.

Important though he was, he never let you feel it and

doing business with him, once you had his confidence, was a rare pleasure. Earlier in his career he had promoted a number of shows at his own risk, but in that field his failures had exceeded his successes and he had lost a lot of money. He never complained, took his misfortunes on the chin and on no occasion was there any doubt about his discharging all his obligations to the last penny. But as a result of his experiences he eventually vowed never to take the risk of an own promotion again. Until one day, his friend and colleague Prince Littler told him that he could offer him a piece of the original production of a musical entitled "My Fair Lady". His immediate reply was, "But you know, I never touch productions any more." Nothing daunted, Prince Littler made it his business to persuade him to make an exception. He told me that the profits from his share considerably exceeded the sum total of all his previous losses.

His client Maria Callas had the reputation of being an unreliable artist und cancelling performances at the last moment. Gorlinsky, as in fact did Lord Harewood who, as director of the Edinburgh Festival had come to know her well, maintained that this was quite untrue; she just did not like signing any documents, but she always stood by her word. That is provided she did not really fall ill, as was the case on her artistically disastrous farewell tour, when more often than not, either she or her partner di Stefano produced large insurance claims against Lloyd's, which incidentally brought to light the fact that she had been suffering from glaucoma for some time, surprisingly without realising it.

Gorlinsky, too, had a good sense of humour, as witnessed by a prominently displayed notice in his office: "If God had wanted us to go to concerts, he would have given us free tickets." He loved his work. As his widow once said, "He went to his office each day like going on holiday."

Last but not least there was the Berlin concert promoter *Luise Wolf,* who, after her husband's death, ran the concert agency Wolf & Sachs, without question the leading firm in Germany prior to the advent of the Nazis. She had originally been an actress and it showed. No wonder her family called her "Königin Luise" after a well-loved German Queen in the 18th century. Her importance can be judged by the fact that she promoted the regular Berlin symphony concert series both of Wilhelm Furtwängler and Bruno Walter. After these concerts, she usually gave a dinner for the performing artists and prominent guests. It was at one of these that the wife of Fritz Kreisler is said to have remarked (long before the ascent of the Nazis, by the way; but being Jewish was, of course, something of a disadvantage even then) "Fritz has actually very little Jewish blood in him". Which prompted one of those present to reply: "Oh, I did not know Fritz is anaemic."

One cannot maintain that Luise Wolf was generally liked by the Berlin musical profession. Once, when she was visiting Venice, somebody asked for her address there; someone else answered: "Just address the letter to "Canaille Grande" and it is bound to arrive safely. In those pre-Hitler days Berlin was the undisputed musical centre in Europe and every beginner had to have a recital in Berlin under his belt, hopefully with favourable press reviews. These concerts would, of course, be very badly attended by paying patrons; the solution was to stuff them with freeloaders and they therefore cost the performers quite some money, including a fat fee for the concert agency arranging the event, thus a very desirable piece of business. Luise Wolf had built up such a high reputation that artists considered it quite prestigious to use her agency. She made it a rule for unknown artists to audition for her before she accepted them, rather a matter of form, for she was a good business woman and not easily willing to forgo any income. Yet she usually managed to make the artist feel that it was not he, but she, who did the favour by accepting the job of arranging the concert. However, to do her justice, she made it a principle to attend these concerts in person or, at least, to appear in the Green Room afterwards. She would work out precisely at what time the concert would finish and thus, not rarely was able to skip the performance itself. The story goes that on one of these occasions she approached the artist with outstretched hands and said enthusiastically *"Noch nicht dagewesen wie Sie gespielt haben"*. I am afraid I have to spoil this untranslatable pun by a laborious explanation. In German, "Noch nicht dagewesen wie Sie gespielt haben" usually means something like "quite unheard of, the mastery of your performance". But literally it can also mean: "I was not yet present when you played". I thought this story to be an invention until I found it repeated in a reliable book describing Berlin concert life, warts and all; so, more likely than not, it is true.

Let us leave musicians for a bit, *Golo Mann*, son of the world-famous Thomas Mann, and subsequently himself a prominent historian and author, though not anything like his super-famous father, was, like myself, a pupil at Salem, the boarding school I am describing elsewhere in this book. He was one or two years my senior, but, notwithstanding the age difference, we became, good friends. Most dormitories at the school consisted of 4 to 8 beds, and for some time I was in the dorm of which he was the head boy. With hindsight, this is somewhat astonishing: well before I had arrived at the school, Golo apparently had had a room to himself. The reason: he had been regarded as having homosexual tendencies. I heard that story, many years after his death, from a German academic who was researching his work and who was able to cite some letters written by the school's headmaster, Kurt Hahn, in which this tendency was being discussed; thus there can be no doubt about the authenticity of this story. Nevertheless, I find it hard to credit. Kurt Hahn had such a panic fear of homosexuality that I doubt he would have allowed Golo to remain at the school had he really been an active homosexual. Yet he must have discovered some such tendency in him. On this score, he should be complimented on his insight into his pupils' psyche; Golo indeed became a homosexual in later life. But when I was at the school, the whole episode, such as it was, was obviously over and done with; I never heard about it, and Golo was entrusted with heading a dormitory, so the school must have considered that the "danger" had passed. Nor did I notice any signs of a homosexual tendency in him. On the contrary, he once talked disapprovingly about his father "liking little boys"; Thomas Mann's sexuality has been the subject of some speculation by his biographers.

Golo was fairly awkward and clumsy in his demeanour, not interested in sport (though he played hockey, I believe in the school's second eleven) and decidedly was not a success with the girls who must have found his company boring if not even a little threatening. I remember him, at a school dance, asking a very pretty and sought-after girl for a dance. She refused, and he turned away with an ironic remark, which I no longer remember, except that the words "silly goose" appeared in it.

There can be no doubt that Thomas Mann's immense fame must have been a heavy burden for Golo; he suffered from the "famous father syndrome" with a vengeance. However, he did not give up the uneven struggle but became a rebel instead, no doubt at home as well as, to my certain knowledge, at the school where he got involved in many clashes with the school authorities. I found it amusing that, many years later, he had completely changed his spots. The occasion was an important school anniversary at which he was the main speaker. He made a most laudatory speech about Kurt Hahn and the school, distinctly though no doubt unintentionally mirroring his father's style.

Thomas Mann must himself have been somewhat ambivalent towards his son. One of the most impressive memories of my school days is the arrival of the family Mann, Thomas, his wife, and their two youngest children at Salem, where he read to us, very well, his delightful, partly autobiographical short story "*Unordnung und frühes Leid*", which at the time had not yet been published in book form. The remarkable fact about it was that Mann had six children (in three pairs with distinct intervals between each pair), but in the story had mentioned only four. Golo and his sister Monica, the second pair, were left out. This cannot have failed to have registered with Golo.[5]

He once acted, and very well too, in the title role of Schiller's "*Wallensteins Tod*". I had the honour of playing "opposite" him, as his valet with one line to say. This formed the highlight of my thespian career; my only other appearance having been in a Christmas school play, in which I played the part of a landlord refusing shelter to Mary and Joseph. Unfortunately, Mary, at the decisive moment, forgot her lines and left me standing there, rather forlornly. This led me to the conclusion early-on that the acting profession was not for me.

Golo once came to stay with me at my parents' home in Baden-Baden. The event has stuck in my memory: he was given to very ironic remarks, and on the day of his visit, the local paper had reported the arrival in Baden-Baden of the world-famous violinist Fritz Kreisler. "Well", were almost his first words to me "what does your father feel about that, eh?" I was able to reply coolly: "Oh, Mr. and Mrs. Kreisler will be coming to us for supper tonight and there will be some chamber music afterwards." It turned out to be a most memorable evening and Golo was, for once, somewhat gobsmacked.

---

[5]And possibly equally, with Monica, also a pupil at Salem for a few terms. She had a somewhat lively imagination and once ran screaming from the school library, the "*Kapitelsaal*" – Salem had originally been a monastery – because the Abbot Oexle dating back to the 16th century, I believe, had suddenly appeared to her. In later life, she married, to everybody's surprise, a simple fisherman on the Isle of Capri. I cannot help feeling though I have no proof whatsoever, that her family relationships must have had something to do with it. Perhaps a protest?

Incidentally, curiously enough, the youngest son of Thomas Mann became a professional musician and for some time was a pupil of my father. He had a lot of difficulties and was not a very good violinist (nor later viola player as his sonata partner, Yalta Menuhin, once confirmed to me). After my father's death I came across a long letter from him discussing his troubles; the style was an absolute copy of that of Thomas Mann. I still regret that it got lost during World War II.

Thomas Mann had, like many famous people, an intimate (but doubtless entirely non-sexual) relationship with, to my knowledge, a fairly average elderly lady to whom he wrote the most profound letters, of which she was rightly immensely proud. I had met her in London; she was a nice person, undoubtedly intelligent, but seemed to me, to be nothing particularly special. Since I found her stories about this correspondence with Mann somewhat unlikely, I asked Golo at an Alt-Salem meeting about it. "It is true," he said "she was the wall on which my father wrote his graffiti." A telling sign not only of his ability to turn a nice phrase but equally of the dislike, with which the families of famous men usually regard these "interlopers".

To my regret, I lost touch with Golo soon after our schooldays. He once gave a lecture in London which I attended. When I saw him afterwards, he did not, or did not want to, recognise me. There was no reason why he should have felt any hostility towards me, and I am still wondering without chagrin what caused that particular repression. .

Two other children of famous parents were *Karl Ulrich (Karuli)* and *Stefan Schnabel*, sons of the pianist Artur and the singer Therese Schnabel. I have described Artur very fully elsewhere[6]. Therese lost her voice rather early in her career, remained, however, an outstanding and much sought-after teacher. Unfortunately she also made, fairly late, some records with her husband. As far as I am concerned, I find this a regrettable indication of the fact that even the most intelligent artists often do not know when it is time for them to stop. But Therese was a lovely and gentle lady admired by all who knew her.

Karuli was very musical and became a professional pianist. Though he did not reach his father's heights, he was by no means a bad one and certainly not as negligible an artist as many people made him out to be, inevitably comparing him with his famous father. He did not give the

---

[6] "and do you play the violin?".

appearance of suffering from Schnabel senior's fame, though it is bound to have influenced him and his career. He was highly intelligent and had many interests. In his demeanour, he was boyish, enthusiastic, outspoken and idiosyncratic. I remember a party at a mutual friend's house, where he suddenly declared in a loud voice, referring to the widow of a well-known musicologist: "Of course, everybody knows that she murdered him". There was dead silence for a moment, but then apparently everybody decided to disregard this outrageous remark and conversation flowed on as if nothing had happened. Today, I suppose, it could have cost him millions in slander damages, but this was long before the emergence of our present compensation culture.

Through the association of our fathers, we had been friends from early childhood, and remained on close terms until the end of his life. I remember, from my student days, the table tennis parties he gave at weekends at his parents' residence, which was on the top floor of a block of flats. One day the people living underneath it rebelled. They felt that with Artur and Karuli practising and teaching the piano all day and Therese doing likewise with singing, Sunday ought to be a day of rest. I recall that we all found this attitude highly unreasonable.

Stefan, the second son, became an actor. He never achieved real fame, but, after emigration to USA, was for a long time in the cast of a soap opera in which he played the part of a famous surgeon. Eventually there were protests from the public; they considered that he had become far too old for this exacting profession. So they had to kill him off.

During World War II he frequently played small parts in films, as a German officer or spy. When the war ended, I remarked to his parents, somewhat tactlessly "What is Stefan going to do now? I suppose he will have to play Russian members of the KGB." This uncalled-for remark was not at all well received, but, as it turned out, I had been right and in films containing such a part, ten to one you could expect the somewhat sinister-looking Stefan to pop up.

He had a great deal of wit (inherited from his father) and it was he who made the unfortunately abortive suggestion to me that we should appear at a sonata recital of our fathers with placards round our necks, stating "No, I don't play the piano" (or, in my case, the violin); anticipating the inevitable question by strangers, "and do you also play the…"?[7]

Schnabel had a third child, an illegitimate daughter, who unexpectedly turned up in Berlin when she was in her thirties. He had fathered her at the tender age of 15, obviously being a child prodigy not only in music. She was a very lively and charming woman and fully accepted by all the family including Schnabel's wife. She was for some time the girlfriend of the Zionist leader Dr. Nahum Goldman, which did not stop her from occasionally straying. I have nothing but admiration for the State of Israel, but have to say that she was my only active connection with Zionism.

Another good friend was the violinist *Szymon Goldberg*, who became my father's pupil at an early age. I found a copy of a conciliatory and very wise letter from my father to Szymon's previous teacher[8] who had been most upset at losing such a promising pupil. It sheds an interesting light on the varying attitudes in such cases. A really conscientious teacher ought to realise when his pupil has outgrown him. But this is by no means always the case.

As far as I know, a biography about Szymon is in existence, so I will not repeat it here. Although his career started very promisingly – he became first leader of the Berlin Philharmonic Orchestra at a very early age – he never quite reached the absolute heights he deserved, not due to any violinistic failings, but simply because his personality was a little too unassuming and not sufficiently flamboyant. Everybody was surprised, therefore, when he teamed up in a

---

[7] Hence the title of my first book
[8] It is now in the Flesch manuscript collection of the Nederland's Muziek Instituut, The Hague

sonata duo with the very outgoing and assertive Schnabel pupil Lily Kraus, though the difference in temperament does not seem to have been a bar to the ensemble's success.

He was married to a charming lady, older than he, with whom he had started an affair in his teens. I remember my mother telling me that this lady had remarked to a mutual friend: "I know this wonderful relationship cannot last, but I am enjoying it to the full while it does." Instead they married and stayed together for many years until her death in old age after a long illness.

After her death he moved to Japan and married, he must have been around 80, a young Japanese pianist. He had a delightful sense of humour and I am sure will forgive me, if I relate that he once sent me a programme of a recital he had given with her. On it was a photo of the pair and I realised that the lady in question was exceedingly pretty. I was just about to write congratulating him on having married such an attractive wife, when I came to the conclusion that it was impossible for a woman with such good looks to marry so old a man. I was wrong, she was the one, and it was an absolute love match. I met her after his death when, as an act of devotion, she made it her business to undertake a sentimental journey to all the places at which he lived during his long life.

A highly interesting man was *Georg Bernhard*, for many years chief editor of the Berlin *"Vossische Zeitung"*, equivalent, say, to the "Guardian" today. He was also an MP and a professor at the *Handelshochschule*, the Berlin equivalent to the LSE. No wonder that he was a very prominent man in political as well as social circles. Our families happened to be good friends and my father played not infrequently at house concerts in the Bernhard home. His assessment of Bernhard in a diary entry sums the man up:

"Peculiar mixture of clear thinking and adventurous phantasising (very noticeable in his bidding when playing cards[9]). If he were not to act the proletarian in such a pronounced and to many people convincing, way, but showed more dignity and exchanged the role of the son of the earth for something more fitting his position, he would probably by now be Chancellor of the Exchequer".

On his 50th birthday his staff issued a private edition of his paper, dealing of course entirely with him. One of the ads in it has stuck in my memory: "Will any clairvoyant who has not yet been consulted by a gentleman with greying hair and a lighted cigar, kindly contact the editorial office of this paper immediately."

Bernhard was certainly not infallible. In fact I was present when he uttered in 6 (in English translation 7) words the most misguided opinion I have ever heard or hope to hear. When during the early days of the Nazi regime, after a concert given by my father (which at that time was still possible[10]) the families sat together in a Berlin restaurant, the news came through on the wireless that the Reichstag was on fire. This prompted Bernhard to say: "This is the end of the Nazis". We were all highly pleased to hear such an optimistic opinion from a man who had the best information and assessments imaginable. In fact, of course, the fire was practically the real beginning of the Third Reich.

Of course, Bernhard lost his job shortly afterwards and emigrated. I lost sight of him, but as far as I know he never

---

[9] When my father invited friends to play Skat, probably the most popular German card game at the time, the wives of the participants usually went together to the theatre or a cinema. Bernhard lost at cards with monotonous regularity. Shortly before the return of the ladies, he usually suggested that they should settle up. Thereafter they would continue playing and when the ladies returned from their outing, his wife (who incidentally had been a dentist, a rarity in those days) would ask him: "Well, are you losing heavily as usual?" Bernhard was then able to show her a practically clean score card.

[10] and which, as a matter of fact, is mentioned by the writer Lion Feuchtwanger in his famous novel "Die Familie Oppenheim". However, the passage is niot very flattering to him: the heroine is asked to go to this concert and declines as not being sufficiently interesting.

attained anything like his previous position.

He had an attractive daughter. When I was about eight and she probably five, somebody suggested to her that she should marry me. She graciously consented, though on one condition: that I provided her with a bathroom with steps leading into the bath, in her eyes obviously the height of refinement. It took me over 85 years before I could comply with her request: I replaced my bath with a shower cabinet, to enter which two steps are required. But by then we had lost touch and it was impossible to remind her of her promise. Life is full of disappointments.

Benno Elkan was a sculptor who had emigrated from Hitler Germany. His main work so far had been the famous German *"Freiheitsdenkmal"* which the Nazis promptly destroyed. In London, he specialised in religious themes. Two of his candelabras are in Westminster Abbey, and his main work, a giant *Menorah*, stands in front of the *Knesset* in Jerusalem. It had been commissioned by the House of Commons. Elkan was a client of mine and I insured this candelabra from its earliest stage. His studio was in a street with heavy traffic, with the result that his work, initially of course in clay, was several times partly ruined by the vibrations caused by passing buses and lorries... As he was insured against that contingency, it is true to say that a large part of the work was paid for by Lloyd's. I was present at the ceremony of dedication in the House and remember sitting opposite a lady with particularly nice legs. From later photos I realised that she had been the, at that time still fairly unknown Barbara Castle.

When, after the war, the Guildhall School of Music launched the Carl Flesch International Violin Competition, I agreed to provide the medal for the winner and commissioned Elkan to sculpt it. My father was to be depicted on it in profile, but try as I might, I could not locate a profile picture but only *en face* photos. When the medal was ready, I was absolutely astounded by the accuracy of the profile Elkan had constructed from this scanty material. It proved his outstanding technical artistry.

Back to music. I have written elsewhere;[11] about *Hans Keller* (as have many others), but one or two stories deserve repetition. He was one of the most important musicologists of his time, responsible *inter alia* for many years for much of the BBC's Radio 3 programmes. In this capacity he once constructed a tape of entirely meaningless electronic music and broadcast it as the work of an imaginary composer whom he called Zak. Those radio critics who wrote about it (and did of course not know that it was a hoax), panned it mercilessly. For a member of the old generation for whom contemporary compositions are almost without exception meaningless, it is interesting that it is indeed possible to distinguish between good and bad modern music, a sign of the unstoppable development that leaves us oldies behind. What eventual influence will this have on the classic repertoire?

Keller had arrived in this country as a penniless Jewish refugee from Austria and initially earned his living partly as a reader and editor for a firm of publishers. In this capacity he translated and, together with me, edited my father's posthumous memoirs[12], adding numerous learned footnotes. When it came to a technical assessment of the famous violinist Bronislav Huberman, whose playing my father had greatly disliked, but whom Keller venerated, he added a very long footnote proving, at least to his own satisfaction, that my father had been disastrously wrong. I demurred: "I cannot judge the pros and cons, but this is my father's book; if you want to write about Huberman at that length, publish your own book." Crisis! Neither of us would give in. Eventually we came to a compromise, to my knowledge almost unique in publishing history: Keller would give his opinion in an appendix, and I would write a reply. When Keller read my piece, he exclaimed: "Not good enough" and rewrote it in much stronger terms. It was typical of the man, he held strong

---

[11] "and do you also play the violin?"....
[12] "Carl Flesch memoirs"

opinions, from which he would not budge, but at the same time he was anxious that the opposing views should be expressed in the most adequate manner.

Another field, in which he excelled was, of all things, that of football pools. He brought his wonderfully analytical mind to bear on them and regularly won prizes. I asked him repeatedly to let me participate in his forecasts, but he always refused; he did not want to carry the responsibility of losing my money, should his opinion be proved wrong.

His premature death was tragic and a great loss to all his friends and admirers.

Another man who left us far too early was the political cartoonist Victor Weiss who during the immediate after-war years became almost a household word under his pen name *Vicky*. It shows the ephemeral nature of fame. During his life time, there can have been few people who had not heard of him and enjoyed his work; today the mention of his name evokes hardly a flicker of recognition.

He, too, was a Jewish Hitler refugee. I must have been one of the very first, if not the first, who gave him a commission, a Christmas card for my insurance firm in the form of a caricature of myself and bearing the message: "C F Flesch ASSURES you of his best wishes". It took him exactly five minutes to do. His fee was 2 guineas, £2.10.

He was a client of my insurance firm. When it came to his household insurance, he mentioned that his housekeeper, a refugee from, I believe, Yugoslavia, had some jewellery; was this covered by his insurance? There were several firms of jewellers who carried out appraisals for insurance purposes free of charge (they made their money in the form of replacement orders when one of the insured items got lost) and I suggested a valuation. When this arrived at my office, it read something like this:

"1 pearl necklace £10.
1 brooch £15.
1 wristwatch £12.

49

1 pair of earrings £5,000" (the equivalent today of about £100,000).

I rang up the firm and pointed out the typing error. "No, it's quite correct; the earrings caused a sensation in our shop." Obviously, the girl, coming from a very wealthy family, had had no idea of the value. So I rang Vicky: "I have an excellent offer for your housekeeper's ear rings, £300"? "Oh yeah? They are already in a bank safe."

Like so many funny and witty professionals, he was basically a tragic figure and suffered from severe bouts of depression which eventually led to his suicide. Had he survived, I would have suggested to him a cartoon for the day after Winston Churchill's death: Valhalla. Shakespeare, Nelson and Wellington standing in a group looking down to earth on Churchill, waving, cigar in hand, and just about to commence his upward journey. Shakespeare to the others: "Winston's back!" Oh, sorry, I forget, most of today's readers probably don't get the point: "Winston is back" was the famous signal by the Royal Navy when, immediately at the outbreak of World War II, Churchill was appointed First Lord of the Admiralty. His time as the supreme war leader was still to come, but even so, his appointment gave us a wonderful feeling of security.

That's it. I hope I have made my point: you do not necessarily have to be, or remain, famous for something interesting or amusing to be said about you. Now let us turn to other matters.

3

How to become a neurotic – and how to get out of it (well – more or less…).

> *"They fuck you up, your mum and dad,*
> *They do not mean to, but they do…".*

Philip Larkin

I have no complaints. By and large, I spent a happy early childhood. My parents were kind and caring, looking after us children very well (albeit with the help of governesses, par for the course at the time) and doing their very best for us, as they saw it. That it did not always turn out as well as they expected and deserved was not their fault.

Initially, I liked school and was a good pupil, but this changed when I was about ten: things started to go wrong, and I began to loathe and fear it. In spite of private coaching. I ended up for much of the time near the bottom of the class, having eventually to repeat one year. Matters improved somewhat when, at the age of 15, I changed to Salem, the well-known German boarding school whose headmaster, Kurt Hahn, subsequently founded Gordonstoun.[13] I was able, mainly by luck, to make up the lost year and eventually to complete my A levels fairly satisfactorily before my 18th birthday. In fact, I was still 17 during my first term at university.

But school was only the beginning of my troubles: one year into my law studies, I developed a fairly severe neurosis, which among other difficulties resulted again in an almost complete inability to do any real work. Eventually matters got

---

[13] See number 8

so bad that I underwent psychoanalysis (as I shall describe later). I cannot say that this gave me an immediate insight into the causes of my difficulties, but I think I have since been able to piece together their main origin: my famous father, the violinist Carl Flesch.

Famous parents are an undoubted problem for most children. When you are little, being the son of an outstanding person is an undiluted pleasure. The fame rubs off on you; you get more than the usual attention from strangers as well as friends of the family who cherish the connection with you, not for your own but your parent's sake. But there is an undoubted reverse side of the coin: it prolongs the conscious as well as subconscious belief in the parent's infallibility. For a baby parents are, of course, all-powerful and all-knowing. Normally, this feeling begins to wear off at quite an early age and the older the child gets, the more it realises that father and mother have their faults and weaknesses too, by no means know everything and can even be outwitted. This is a normal and healthy development leading to an ever-increasing sense of independence. With a famous father, on the other hand, the belief in his immense powers is unduly prolonged. After all, everybody tells you how wonderful he is, and proofs are all around you.[14] Thus, the onset of independence is retarded. The child remains "the son of" or "the daughter of" the famous so-and-so, instead of becoming an individual of its own. And this can be very damaging

---

[14] Of course, there are many different kinds of fame: that of pop stars and footballers who, after a number of years inevitably fade, boxers and athletes who begin getting beaten; and politicians who are violently and viciously attacked by the opposition (I once had an interesting conversation about this with Wolfgang Stresemann whose father, Gustav Stresemann, had been one of the most important and controversial statesmen of the Weimar republic). I am disregarding all these types in the present context, restricting myself to the by and large steady and enduring fame of a widely recognised artist.

indeed.[15]

What are the consequences? Long-term, if you are not careful, this habit of automatically feeding off the position of your parent can accompany you throughout life; I remember the son of the pianist Artur Schnabel once introducing me to an acquaintance with the words: "May I introduce the son of Carl Flesch." We were both in our fifties and both our fathers had long departed this life, but for him the old habit remained. We had been friends since our early childhood, but clearly there was to his mind nothing more interesting about me than that I was the son of a famous musician.

This can be pretty ridiculous, but harmless. One often embarrassing by-product, though, is the reference to the famous father if the person to whom you are being introduced, has no idea who the famous man really was. Very awkward both for the other person and "the son of" himself. I wish, people wouldn't do it.

But I digress. Other more immediate consequences of the father's outstanding position can be far more serious. There are in my view three possible reactions on the part of the son, once he has absorbed the outstanding position of the parent. If he has a strong personality, he will go his own independent way or possibly even try to emulate the parent in, as it were, "peaceful combat" and without a feeling of animosity. This, of course, is the best possible option, only available to the offspring who can successfully deal with his

---

[15] The pianist Moritz Rosenthal, famous in the first half of the 20th century not only for his art, but also for his wit, hit the nail on the head when he wrote into my sister's autograph album "To Hanni Flesch, the charming daughter of the famous violinist Carl Flesch – and herself."

parent's fame.[16] Alternatively, his original admiration may turn on its head and develop into an intense and open hostility. Sometimes he goes public with it. There are some examples of "Mother Dear" type books showing this tendency to a marked and usually distasteful degree.

And lastly the son can, without, of course, consciously realising it, come to the conclusion, that there is nothing comparable to what the father does, and that he will never be able to do anything similarly worthwhile – so why try? That means that he gives up the unequal struggle. This again can take different forms: he may become a drunkard, a junkie or worse. Alternatively his reaction may be simply passive.

No doubt, the latter is what happened to me, although neither I nor anybody else realised it at the time. I was fairly musical and it was obvious that I should learn to play an instrument. I chose the piano; it never occurred to me to try the violin, this was, subconsciously, entirely out of my reach. But even piano playing gave me no pleasure and, to my subsequent eternal regret, I gave it up. Similarly, there was nothing else in any other field that seemed remotely to compare with what my father did. So I simply refused to learn and my school reports were abysmal. Since I was quite intelligent, this defied rational explanation, for at that time, in the early 1920s, child psychology was largely a thing of the future. So nothing was done except scolding.

Initially, after I had changed over to the boarding school, Salem, the situation did not change. Although I was repeating the same form, I was easily the worst pupil in class, so much so that a whole committee of teachers began to pay attention to my case and took me to task. Asked for the reason of my outstandingly poor performance, I said the first thing that

---

[16] A good example is the violinist Igor Oistrakh, son of the legendary David. I met him when he was a member of the jury at the International Carl Flesch Violin Competition and asked him how his father's fame had affected his career. I expected the moan one so often hears in these cases, but instead he said "wonderfully!" which left me somewhat gobsmacked.

came into my head. "Since I am repeating the class, I know it all already, and it bores me." To my surprise, they swallowed that and decided to put me into the next-higher form. For no good reason that I can see, this proved to be a turning point. With some one-to-one tutoring I was able to catch up, and whilst I was never an outstanding scholar, managed to hold my own.

This marked the end of what I may call the first phase of my neurosis. Unfortunately, it returned with redoubled strength during my student days. Not only was I unable, again, to do any work, but I became the victim of various anxieties, not least claustrophobia as well as agoraphobia – you name it.

So much for the "history". But let me look at the relationship with my father a little more closely. It was not that I was "in awe" of him in the sense that I feared him. On the contrary, I greatly liked his company and felt comfortable in it. He exuded absolute authority without any apparent effort. During my boyhood I very rarely doubted his wisdom and judgement. If his views did not accord with mine, I automatically concluded that I must be in the wrong.

Not that he spent a great deal of time with us children, he was a very busy man, quite apart from the fact that he was away on concert tours a good deal. And I accepted fully that his work was far more important than we were[17]. This opinion was ingrained in me, so much so that, when I happened to visit the house of a classmate and occasionally observed that his father was far more involved with him than mine was with me, my genuine reaction was not, as one might have expected, envy but the immediate, possibly even slightly contemptuous thought – "has this man nothing more important to do than to play with his children?" This feeling

---

[17] There was a saying in our family – jocular, and recognised by us children as such – "in case of fire, first the violin, then the children". When I once innocently quoted this to acquaintances they were, to my utter surprise, horrified. We had never found anything wrong with it.

is in marked contrast to that of children who claim as grown-ups that they suffered in their youth from the fact that their famous father (or mother) did not spend sufficient time with them. I doubt that, in many instances, this feeling is genuine. A case in point is that of Yehudi Menuhin's children who have gone into print (or was it a film?) expressing this sentiment quite strongly. I don't believe it for one moment, if only because Yehudi, a lovely personality quite apart from his violinistic genius, travelled all the year round and this must have been a way of life for his children from their birth onwards; hence they cannot have consciously "suffered" through the lack of something they never had or expected. However, I do not intend to psychoanalyse the subconscious motives of Yehudi's children. I have sufficient to do with my own.

Incidentally, it is by no means certain how much time parents *should* really spend with their children. Cases of kids who dread their parents' visits to their school, are well-known. They fear that the father or mother might commit a *faux pas* permanently damaging their own reputation in the eyes of their peers. I know of a case in point: an acquaintance told me proudly that he and his wife had visited their son every weekend at his boarding school. Many years later the son told me how much he had dreaded these visits. I even know of two cases where the children were deeply ashamed of their father. His crime? He was much older than the fathers of most of their friends.

My own father was a reserved man who could best express his feelings through his music. One of his diary entries is significant: "My feelings for my pupils are those of a father, and *like him* (my italics) it is not given to me to show them openly". I never missed this – especially as my mother could be very affectionate – for there was at no time any doubt that he cared deeply for all his family.

At any rate, whatever the rights and wrongs of the situation, things had come to a pass where outside help was definitely called for. For me, it came by way of psychoanalysis.

At that time Freud was, of course, still alive and – more important, for he himself was already severely handicapped by throat cancer – most of his original pupils were active and in full swing. Analysis was still a comparatively young science, which as well as the pros and cons of the different schools, such as Adler and Jung that had been founded in competition were the subjects of heated debates.

In some professional circles psychoanalysis was not regarded as a science at all. Today its detractors' main argument seems to be that it has been overtaken by more modern methods and that time has, in any case, shown that many of Freud's theories were mistaken and have been disproved. Though I am, other than by personal experience on the couch, in no way qualified to judge this, I find that assertion pretty questionable. Originally psychoanalysis was attacked as entirely unproven and un–provable, and now the same schools of psychology (not of course the same practitioners) pronounce it as outdated. Logically, for a theory to be outdated, there must have been a time during which it had been regarded as valid, but in the case of analysis, this small link seems, in the minds of its opponents, to be missing. A curious state of affairs, which must mean something. Freud, of course, had a ready answer: the more the subconscious mind rejects and suppresses something as too near the knuckle, the fiercer the conscious opposition and the greater, therefore, the proof of its validity. This may be so, but to me it always seemed to be a facile argument by which you can prove *anything* to your own satisfaction.

Yet there is little doubt that emotional factors, not to mention anti-Semitism, did play a part in its rejection by the orthodox psychiatric schools who sometimes went to ridiculous lengths in their efforts to discredit it. This went so far as somebody (I forget where I read it) "proving" that Freud had even chosen the wrong name for his method: he should not have called it "psychoanalysis", but "psychanalysis". Someone else, when referring to Freud's book analysing humour, upbraided him for the poor quality of the jokes he had chosen. With this, as a matter of fact, I tend to agree, but it is, of course, completely beside the point, since their sole purpose was to illustrate his theories, not to make his readers laugh.

We youngsters, as far as we were interested in the subject, swallowed analysis hook, line and sinker. I remember a student ball, in Heidelberg, a public event, which featured a kiosk selling cigarettes (at that time of course more than fully acceptable: a social necessity). The slogan on that kiosk read: "The cigarette is not only a sexual symbol, you can also smoke it!" We read Freud avidly without the remotest chance of understanding him, though not everybody would admit to that. The one exception for me was his "Psychopathology of Everyday Life" ("Psychopathologie des Alltagslebens"), which was comparatively easy to grasp and showed what a wonderfully gifted and lucid writer he was in addition to his other achievements.

I had come across psychoanalysis purely by chance: one of my co-students and friends at Heidelberg University was the son of the late Karl Abraham who had been one of Freud's foremost pupils. His widow still maintained close connections with many of his former colleagues, a few of whom I met at her home in Berlin. When my neurosis began disturbingly to manifest itself, I consulted one of them, Theodor Reik, another leading Freud pupil. (He should, incidentally, not be confused with his still more famous colleague Wilhelm Reich). As a student, I did not, of course, have any income of my own and my father had, a short time previously, lost all his money and his beloved violin in the New York stock exchange crash of 1929. He did his best to divert me towards the simpler, quicker and therefore cheaper method of Alfred Adler's "Individual Psychologie" (one of whose practitioners he happened to know) but I, of course, "knew better" and would not be diverted from my wish to undergo analysis. Needless to say, neither he nor I knew anything about either method. As I said, my connection with psychoanalysis was purely accidental; had I, as a student, met the son of an Adlerian or Jungian practitioner, I have no doubt that I would have become an ardent follower of that school. I have never ceased to acknowledge with astonished gratitude my father's very considerable financial sacrifice to humour me at a time when he himself went through a most severe financial crisis. I think it underlines what I already said about his character, never mind what unintended adverse influence he had on my psyche.

Not infrequently, former analysis patients are either fanatical adherents or implacable enemies of the method. Part of the reason is that transference between analyst and patient is by its very nature both close and ambivalent; the severance can be traumatic and cause a somewhat illogical state of mind. Reik once told me that one of his patients, who had undergone a successful course of treatment, but had hated ending it, subsequently declared with full conviction that the disappearance of his symptoms had by no means been the result of the analytic treatment, but had been caused by his taking, of all things, a laxative afterwards. I myself can claim a more detached view. Analysis is a very interesting experience, helping you, and I suspect to a greater extent than any other method, to recognise and accept your subconscious motivations, even if not exactly to understand them. This enables you to deal with them more easily, more effectively and in particular without unnecessary guilt feelings. It can be an ongoing process. I myself, long after having completed my treatment (not a full cure – I believe this is impossible with *any* method) have found it beneficial from time to time to have, as it were, "a further piece" of analysis, a refresher if you like.

Incidentally, treatment takes a shorter time, the younger the age at which it is commended. But, of course, as is clear from my own case, parents very rarely recognise the signs in their own children. They will regularly have their teeth and eyes checked, make sure that they do not have flat feet and if the children are lucky, insist on a healthy diet. But God forbid that this should extend to psychological aspects! Having myself been taught by experience, I later insisted, overcoming my wife's objections with some difficulty, on having both my children looked at by an experienced analyst at the Anna Freud Institute at an early age, in order to ascertain whether there were any signs of neurosis that should be nipped in the bud. After three sessions the analyst declared that there appeared to be no need whatever for treatment, incidentally a significant pointer to the lack of avarice of which members of this profession are so frequently accused. I shall briefly return later to this point. One thing is certain: these sessions, provided they are conducted with the necessary professional skill, can have no adverse effect on the child itself. My son, aged about 10, was invited for lunch at a friend's house, and afterwards excused himself: he had to keep a doctor's appointment. "What is wrong?" asked his friend's mother with some concern. "Oh, nothing serious, only the head."

This said, I have to admit that as a purely therapeutic method, psychoanalysis has to be adjudged as somewhat impractical in all but a minority of cases. This has several reasons. Whilst it is capable of achieving a great deal, it takes far too long and is therefore unaffordable to most people. Secondly, analysts of the orthodox Freudian school will hardly ever give advice and guidance in practical terms, but adopt a wholly passive role waiting for the patient to improve sufficiently to arrive at the solutions himself. They just help bringing subconscious feelings into the open, when, in the fresh air of the day, they will disappear by themselves. This, whilst probably correct in theory, is in my view not the best method for a young and inexperienced person who moreover does not know where he is really going. I am by no means certain that more hands-on methods, might not achieve favourable results more quickly, never mind their comparative superficiality.

Theodor Reik, with whom I discussed this question when my father's efforts to make me change over to the

Adler method were at their height, expressed it humorously: "If you have only little money, go to an Adler, if you have sufficient means, go to a Freud analyst." Had I been less self-centred, this ought to have been, in the circumstances, a sufficient reason to change to Adler forthwith. But to my shame, it did not occur to me. Reik's opinion may sound extraordinarily cynical, but it was, of course, not meant that way. It simply reflected the Freudians' view that there were methods, which could superficially show good results, but for a treatment in real depth, psychoanalysis was unmatched. This is no doubt so, but I feel that in many cases a more superficial method with good and quick results is probably sufficient, if only because it usually tends to provide the patient with realistic advice in addition. However this does not mean that apart from my selfishness, I regret the experience as such; analysis gave me great and valuable insights that were of considerable help to me in later life.

I have already referred to the fact that analysts are often regarded as money grabbing and accused of using their undoubted influence over their patients to milk them for all they are worth. In my professional life as an insurance broker I had quite a few analysts as clients whose financial circumstances I could therefore judge to some extent. I am quite certain that, excepting of course charlatans and black sheep whom you will find in any profession, this accusation is unjustified. And this, quite apart from their professionalism, for a very simple reason: an analytic session takes usually 50 minutes with 10 minutes rest for the analyst between patients. The number of patients he can see is therefore of necessity limited. He simply does not have the practical opportunities of coining money in the same way in which some consultants in other specialised fields do, who charge enormous fees after sometimes seeing a patient for only a few minutes, not to mention those like skin specialists whose patients, as the saying goes, are never cured (and never call them out at night either). I had a good illustration of Reik's attitude: in our preliminary interview he said: "In my view, you can overcome your difficulties eventually yourself without analysis. But why waste a lot of energy on something that, with proper help, can be accomplished so much more easily and thoroughly than by DIY methods?"

Of course, analysts are as human and imperfect as the rest of us. Reik was no exception. He was a prolific author and wrote many profound books. But I cannot say that I found his marketing methods always commendable. I once discovered on a railway book stall a paperback by him with the title "The Unknown Murderer" with a lurid cover, bloody footprints in the snow, if I remember rightly, to match. But it was not a crime thriller at all, but dealt with weighty analytical questions and was no doubt entirely beyond the understanding of laymen; I have never ceased to pity the unsuspecting travellers who expected a good read and had a thoroughly spoilt journey instead. I upbraided him about this in one of our sessions, but he showed no contrition.

More important, I myself had quite a traumatic experience of his pragmatism. He had originally been practising in Vienna, but had had the misfortune of one of his patients committing suicide whilst under treatment. Since he was not a medical doctor – not a requirement for psychoanalysts, however stringent their training in other respects – the Austrian authorities had threatened to prosecute him for charlatanry. He had therefore left Vienna and resettled in Berlin. (Incidentally, Freud made Reik's case the subject of a treatise strongly defending "lay analysis" as it is called, and I think he makes a good case). After a few years the Austrian difficulty had apparently died down and there was no longer a risk of prosecution. In consequence, Reik decided to return to Vienna, This must have affected a number of his patients to quite some extent. No doubt he saw to replacements where he found it necessary. In my case, however, he did not see the need – a great mistake since my treatment was by no means completed and I was in the middle of my final university law exams, as stressful an experience as can be imagined. Eventually he did refer me to a colleague, Dr. Hilde Maas, for whose help in a very difficult situation I have been profoundly grateful all my life. She charged me nothing, relying on my promise to pay her when I could. Later, we both happened to have emigrated to London and it gave me particular satisfaction to repay her, when my means allowed it, at a time when she no doubt needed the money far more than she had in Berlin.

I suspect that my case, and possibly that of other patients, gave Reik subconscious problems: Many years later I read a book by him, "Listening with the Third Ear", in which he described his return to Vienna, but put it one year later than it had actually taken place´. There could be no possible error on my part, you don't forget the year in which you sit for your university finals. A case of repression caused by subconscious guilt feeling if ever there was one. Shortly after WWII I looked him up 'purely for old times' sake' in New York where he had settled after the advent of Hitler. I mentioned the matter of the dates to him, but there was absolutely no visible reaction – a nice example, if you like, of how people who have been analysed can deal with their less acceptable subconsciously motivated actions. Or it may have been his professional training, never to evaluate patients' factual statements as such other than in relation to their psyche. I once asked him: "If I were to tell you that I had seen your wife entering a sleazy hotel on the arm of a good-looking young man, what would you do?" "Analyse it" he replied stoutly. I didn't believe him then and don't believe him now. I only hope for his sake that the occasion never arose in which he had to prove his professional detachment in this way.

At the time of my New York visit Reik had built up a successful practice, but had become an old man and no longer the look-alike of the famous conductor Erich Kleiber he had once been, in not very good health and clearly quite worried about it. I could no longer recall or even understand the enormous influence he once had had over me – perhaps an indication of the success of the analytic method.

It would be surprising if during the last 75 years psychiatric science and analysis itself had not undergone considerable changes and improvements. The partial adaptation of the classical analysts' original passive treatment methods that has, I understand, taken place since, is no doubt one of them. To deny for that reason the immense value of Freud's life's work is as ridiculous as to deride the original achievement of anaesthesia because doctors no longer use the original crude method of a nauseous suffocating mask to make a patient unconscious, but give him an injection instead, with the same result. Freud was a genius who advanced psychiatry probably by a century, but he was not the final answer. There never will be in science as long as there are new generations of scientists with enquiring minds.

*

4

Constitutional Monarchy or an elected head of state?

"Elections are won chiefly because most people vote
against somebody rather than for somebody."

Franklin P. Adams

"The senator's victory was a triumph for democracy.
It proves that a multimillionaire has just as
good a chance as everybody."

Bob Hope

When, like me, you come to a country as an asylum-seeking immigrant, you tend to embrace its institutions to the fullest extent. It is not surprising, therefore, that most refugees from Nazi oppression, who entered Great Britain in the 1930s, were admirers of the British monarchy. We all had seen what both a republic and a dictatorship could lead to. And the older ones among us, who had consciously experienced the pre–1918 German monarchy, fully realised the fundamental differences between the German and the British institutions. We were therefore somewhat surprised, even dismayed, when we discovered that there were anti-monarchist feelings among the British population. There is no doubt that they became stronger during the past few decades, culminating in the reaction to the Princess Diana tragedy.

After the 50th Jubilee of Queen Elizabeth II many people thought that that particular episode was now firmly a thing of the past and that from now on the British attitude would, for the foreseeable future, revert to a thoroughly monarchist one. Some months later the collapsed trials of the two royal butlers and the scandalous rumours they caused, proved this expectation to have been unjustified.

The string of Diana books, stories and allegations (even that of her having been murdered by her family) is not likely to diminish and the effect of the whole affair on the monarchy cannot be fully assessed even now. Some time ago, a light-hearted BBC poll resulted in the Prince of Wales achieving the doubtful distinction of, I believe, coming fourth in the list of people members of the public would like to see deported from Great Britain. Well, we don't have to take that seriously, but it might not be amiss to give some renewed thought to the whole question, even if the thoughts are only those of a naturalised Brit.

I can't help feeling that the arguments of both factions often miss the point, as I shall try to demonstrate. May I say from the outset that I remain a convinced supporter of the constitutional monarchy as practised in Great Britain, *as an institution,* though not necessarily of all its royal "executives". But I hope I can claim that my views are objective, governed, as I believe they are, by logic.

Let me first deal with the theory that an elected head of state would be a far better solution than hereditary succession. *"The New Statesman"*, for instance, called the present system in an article on the occasion of the Queen's jubilee "an hereditary institution left stranded in a meritocratic society". Hereditary institution obviously, but could one really call our society meritocratic? A society, whose whole press (as far as I can recall, without exception) knew no better than to make "Beckham's Foot" the top headline on the day after his successful penalty during a football world cup match; a society that adulates, without really valid reasons, pop stars, TV personalities, "Big Brothers" and similar people and values them above practically most persons whose merits are so obviously based on far firmer ground; a society that is prepared to drop its icons just as suddenly when their powers wane (what price now "Beckham's foot"?) or when someone or something else equally silly takes its fancy; a society that professes to so deep a distrust of politicians that an increasing part of the population does not bother to vote at all and where many of those who do and give their trust to their elected representatives become disillusioned with them often within less than a year for reasons no better than those for which they had elected them in the first place – or not infrequently simply because they have become bored with them; a society some (and not just a handful, even though, hopefully, a minority) of whose members, had they but had the chance to do so, would quite likely have supported the crazy notion of the Prince of Wales giving up his claim to the throne (because he allegedly mistreated his wife – what of Henry VIII?) and the tragic and damaged Princess Diana becoming "Regent" until the young Prince William (about whom nobody knew, and still really does not know, anything except that he is good-looking) had come of age? I could go on and on, but I don't think it is necessary. Could these people really be said to give us any confidence in their qualification or ability to elect their head of state on reasonable grounds, let alone "merit"? This, incidentally, is one of the reasons why I am against any idea of every citizen being compelled by law to vote at elections. What can be the possible value of a vote by people who are wholly disinterested, don't want to know anything about these matters and some of whom are highly antisocial themselves? Get real!

But there is more, of course. It is, for instance, an undeniable, however little recognised, fact that "the people" have actually very little say in the election of a head of state, whatever they might be told to the contrary. All they have is the oh so limited Hobson's choice between the two or three candidates put forward, even if no longer after deals in "smoke filled rooms", by the top political players (whom, as we have seen, many distrust), their moneyed patrons and their spin doctors for reasons that often have very little relation to actual merit and even less to the public good. This cannot possibly be called real choice. The inevitable horse trading that goes on behind the scenes ought to be sufficient by itself to discredit this particular system in the eyes of all thinking people.

And look at the election campaigns themselves, not least in the United States. Can the razzmatazz really contribute anything to a rational decision, forgetting even the fact how very undignified it is? An election where the five-o'clock shadow or sweaty brow of one contestant on TV may have swayed thousands of voters? Is it not more likely, as experience has shown in a goodish number of cases, that not only the wrong persons are put before the public, but that the winner (if he is indeed the real winner, which is sometimes hotly disputed) is not even likely to be the best of that poor limited bunch? No – the democratically elected president as the best popular choice is to a large extent an illusion, and a very dangerous one at that.

Still, you might say, right or wrong, it is, after all, "the will of the people". But that is not really true either. The number of votes for successful candidates in Great Britain and the winning majority of American states selecting the leader rarely equals the popular majority. But even when it does, little more than 50 % of the votes will have been in favour of the person elected. And, mark you, this is only the majority of those who bothered to vote. Thus, assuming 80% of the population voted (an almost impossibly optimistic assumption), and there was a majority of 55%, this would mean that the votes in favour were only 44%: a minority whichever way you look at it. The others either did not care or preferred someone else.

And yet another thing: the promoters of each candidate in their turn did their best to convince the voting population that the other candidates, including the one who was eventually elected, were unsuitable, held entirely wrong opinions, proposed the wrong policies, had made promises they knew they could not keep and were possibly even sleazy if not downright corrupt. In brief, they had been doing everything they could to discredit the winner. Sometimes, elections are called "dirty", but as a matter of fact *every* election has to be "dirty" by its very nature. Thus, every elected head of state, is with very few exceptions, anything but the universally recognised "best" person; a very large number of people think the exact opposite. Not an ideal basis for choosing a leader who is supposed to represent the whole nation and behind whom everyone is supposed to unite,

True, you might reply, but this is unavoidable in a democratic society and applies to every parliamentary election. I will not dwell on the differences, such as that the candidates for parliament are put forward, usually after a public or at least semi-public competitive selection procedure and a show of hands by persons who, to some extent at least, represent the people; and further, that, in a way, there is safety in numbers: the voters do not elect only one, but several hundred representatives. I agree that in a democracy a different system of election is not feasible, for parliament that is, but not for the head of state, especially if there is a viable alternative. I am not, of course, advocating that all republics should change into constitutional monarchies. This would be ludicrous. But conversely, I maintain that no useful purpose would be served by adopting the opposite course.

I think I have shown that the popular election of the president or whatever we might call him (or her) is so full of flaws that we might just as well leave matters as they are, a constitutional monarchy, since here a great many of the flaws I have shown up, do not exist.

Of course, there are many faults in a hereditary system as well. An entirely unsuitable person may be the next king or queen. But it undeniably does away with all the unpleasant and undignified by-products of the election process I have just mentioned. And, except in a revolution, which in this country happily seems extremely unlikely, the citizens have no chance of being openly divided. This is an enormous plus point, because it makes it much easier to unite the nation, or a very large part of it, behind the head of state with very few unwarranted allegations being made against the candidate for the simple reason that there is no "candidate".

Yet the monarchic system is in the opinion of some people so deeply flawed that almost anything else would be preferable. So, let us now look at the institution itself a little more closely, warts and all, and see where this leads us.

There is one fallacy of which we should dispose right away: it is often said that the monarchy costs "the taxpayer" enormous amounts of money. I have never heard, though, that taxes were increased because of it or would be reduced if it were abolished. As a matter of fact, compared with other expenditures, it is by no means all that substantial; and the tourist trade it attracts probably pays for a large part anyway. We also overlook that part of it is being paid for by the Royal Family itself. But disregarding all that, would the adequate maintenance of an elected head of state come so much cheaper? I doubt it; it might even be more costly. Elected heads of state are apt to develop expensive tastes and in their case entirely at the State's expense. And let us not forget the saving of the cost of an election both in money and manpower. At any rate, in the question whether we should have a monarchy or not, saving a comparatively negligible amount of money is not and should not be a decisive factor.

As we know, the monarchy being hereditary the succession is predetermined, regardless of merit, and therefore cannot be influenced by the people at all. Call it a flaw if you like. But considering the points I have put forward above, one might just as well call it an advantage. In either case a head of state is often something like a lottery and I see little difference between an unqualified monarch and an unqualified president. And consider this: if the *elected* head of state, being regarded by the world at large, however wrongly, as the true expression of the will and opinions of the country he or she represents, does something disapproved of by most other nations; it is bound to reflect on his country to a far greater extent than the same action by an unelected hereditary monarch. Moreover, the elected head of state has usually far greater powers than the constitutional monarch. If it were different and the head of state had only a purely representative function, why accept all the cost, unpleasantness and hypocrisy of an election for a basically so unimportant post?

The right (such as it is) of Royals to their leading position is largely based on the fact that they are members of the "first" or "highest" family in the land. It may be undesirable to make any such distinctions, but the simple fact is that they do exist and, what is more, are accepted as such by custom and tradition. No-one can really define what characteristics precisely constitute the "best" or "highest". Age? Not really, since, as the former Prime Minister Sir Alec Douglas-Home once so memorably pointed out, there is no difference in the age of any family, high or low. Its known history then? This is rather nearer the mark. Do not many of us play the same game to some extent ourselves? Genealogy is a thriving science or at least hobby in this country. Many of us make every effort to trace our ancestors back as far as possible and are proud and happy if we succeed in unearthing a connection, however remote, with a prominent personage or family of the past. If we can show that they played their part in history, science or art, we certainly are not slow to make this known to all who want to hear it and to many who don't. There is nothing wrong with pride in one's family. It does not, however, make us, the descendants, better people. But that makes usually little, if any, difference in our own eyes or those of our contemporaries. We accept the concept of "leading families" as a fact of life. Then why should we not accept it in the case of a monarch?[18]

I repeat, the members or descendants of any outstanding family, Royals or not, have no right to think that they themselves are better than we ordinary people. But let me point here to a peculiar fact: it is often said that there are royal families who don't give themselves the airs of the British: the bicycle monarchies, so called because the

---

[18] Even the opponents of the monarchy play this game – vide the assertion that the Spencers are a "better" family than the Windsors.

reigning monarch can sometimes be seen cycling through the streets of his or her residence or playing tennis in a not too exclusive club with an "ordinary" citizen. Big deal! Does this really indicate a different character of the institution itself? On the contrary, it seems to me to be a superb PR exercise, whether intended as such or not. It confirms the exalted position of the monarch, but we say, "Look, how marvellous, they act like one of us!" In other words, they are not really one of us, but they do not make us feel it. Why doesn't anybody publish a photo of you, me or one of our friends cycling or playing tennis, even though we (myself excepted!) may be much better at it than the Royal in question? The reason is that, if *we* are doing it, it is not interesting, because we and our families are "ordinary". If a member of the leading family does it, it becomes a matter of public interest by that very fact. It may be that the way in which members of the bicycle royal family behave, changes – ever so slightly – the *face* of the monarchy, but not its character. The way in which we take the Royals' apparently ordinary behaviour on board at its face value is actually one of the strongest proofs of our acceptance that a monarch is a monarch is a monarch, however he or she behaves. And anyway, not all royal families are suitable for the "bicycle treatment". Clearly, the British one isn't, as experience has amply shown. I'll return to this subject presently.

Having said all this, it is still beyond doubt that inherited privilege, like so many things in life must be regarded as unfair and thereby represents a disadvantage of the monarchic system. So, are there any advantages to counteract it? I am, I repeat, referring not to members of the royal family, but to the constitutional monarchy as an institution. One of its main characteristics is that it has to be outside, I am avoiding the word "above", political strife, i.e., that it endeavours to keep entirely non-controversial. Yes, the monarch may be attacked in the press for many reasons, not infrequently in a most rude and unnecessarily offensive manner, but compared with what is constantly being thrown at politicians, including the highest in the land, it is minimal. And the attacks are almost invariably based on personal traits or actions that cannot influence the destiny of the nation in the slightest. This is bound to be conducive to stability, calmness and continuity in a nation. Comparing the political climate in Great Britain and similar monarchies with that in many republican countries during the past 200 years, there can really be no argument about that.

But this is only one of the reasons in favour. There is another. We, the people, need something or someone to look up to. We make pop stars, footballers and similar people our idols, but there can be no doubt that the same applies to a decisively large part of the population in their attitude towards the monarch and many members of the Royal Family. The elevation of pop stars and similar people is to a large extent ephemeral. By contrast, monarchs are a constant factor – they change, with few exceptions, only once or twice in a citizen's life time. Hence they remain people we can look up to for a much longer period than other demigods (if I may use this expression); they cannot be replaced by something new or more interesting, because, by their very nature, they are and remain unique.

Of course, elevating someone to the position of a demigod, can be very detrimental in several respects and not least to the object of the adulation itself. I am firmly convinced that it is bound to change anybody's character for the worse. If you are told every hour of the day that you are better than others; if you are treated accordingly; and if no-one ever contradicts you seriously – you would have to be super-human not to start getting into a state of what I will call "inevitable benign megalomania". It will also tend to lead to the neglect of other persons' feelings. We have dozens of examples for this. The Queen, on one of her famous walkabouts, replying to a woman who expresses pleasure at being able to speak to her, with "You can only speak to me if your are being spoken to first"; the Prince of Wales, invited by a large commercial firm to open its new head office, commiserating in his speech with the people who will have to work in that horrible building; the Duke of Edinburgh telling a boy at a school he visits "You look like a drug addict"; the Queen deciding not to walk to church because of a slightly damaged foot, not bothering to have this announced beforehand to the crowd she knows will be patiently and vainly waiting in the rain. I am convinced that most, if not all, Royals are afflicted with this type of megalomania and gradually become pretty impossible people.

The decisive point is that this condition is benign and not malignant and therefore harmless. More precisely, it does no real damage except to those afflicted by it. And who cares about that? The personage in question does not have the power to make the condition malignant in the sense of influencing events. One of the secrets of the constitutional monarchy's success is that the Royals' characters do not really matter. They may, and do, commit the most appalling gaffes, but this is where it ends. However they live up to these attributes, they do not have the slightest real power enabling them to exercise it to the disadvantage of the people. Everything political is done in the monarch's name, but the decisions are made by others and have to be accepted by him or her as "my Government's", thereby, incidentally, specifically freeing the monarch from responsibility. Thus we have the situation that (a) there are a number of "half-deities", more or less looked up to by everybody as such, however undeservingly, (b) they have been conditioned to believe themselves to be above us ordinary mortals and can therefore become quite unpleasant people; but (c) they have no power to act in accordance with their state of mind and can therefore do next to no harm. What a wonderful solution! A demigod, adulated by a great many people but with no power to do real damage! The ideal lightning conductor. We have only to look at dictatorships, past and present, to realise how catastrophic the opposite can be and usually is: the dictatorial demigods not only believe in their outstanding qualities, they can act accordingly. The rest is history. To my mind this is one of the most striking arguments in favour of the constitutional monarchy.

No doubt the suggestion that the monarch is being looked up to and treated as a demigod will be disputed by many people. And I agree, of course, that hardly anybody consciously realises that they are doing so. But that is just the beauty of it. It cannot be denied that the monarch is beloved by the people purely on the strength of his or her position. Let us again revert to the Queen's Golden Jubilee, which triggered off extraordinary expressions of affection. Fine! But what has the Queen ever really done to justify this opinion? Good deeds? If you disregard the chairmanship of hundreds of Charities (obviously not involving any real work or expense on her part), none that I know of. Is she particularly friendly? I have no idea. I only know her from public appearances on TV where we see her being either kept away from the people or at one of her famous walk-abouts; you only have to look at these to see how perfunctory they are and how they offer no possible opportunity for the people to get on really friendly personal terms with her. Is she particularly intelligent? Could well be, but again I don't know. I cannot recall any profound utterances by her and should I have overlooked any, ten to one they were the work of her script writers; has she made decisions that are good for her people? As we have seen, she can't. The fact is that there is nothing you can put your finger on that stands out as a particular reason for the undoubted love and affection in which she is being held by the people. The same applied to the late Queen Mum whose passing caused general and genuine mourning. As it happens, I was a great admirer of hers: she was of immense value in supporting her weak and inadequate husband, our King during World War II. But this was 60 years ago and is of no interest to the present generation. What did she ever do except smile and wave to the people, speaking a few gracious words to Chelsea Pensioners, and looking much nicer than she probably was? Nothing. Yet wherever the Royals go, they receive the most genuine demonstrations of affection.

A clever PR exercise? To some extent, no doubt. But the most ingenious spin doctors could not generate and maintain this level of genuine, unwavering and constant feeling. We do not "love" the Queen, the "Queen Mum", Prince William as persons but we are loving, without recognising the fact, the institution, the very idea of the monarchy they represent. And there is nothing whatever wrong with that. Most of us play this game. I believe I have made it clear that I do not hold the Royal Family in great esteem. But if I were presented to the Queen, I am sure I would feel proud and honoured in spite of what I have just written. It is the recognition of the institution that counts.

As I said, PR comes into it. But here is a second secret of monarchic success: the mystery surrounding it. Destroy that; make the monarch or members of the Royal Family accessible and thereby as human as in fact they are, and they are in trouble. We have let the people see the monarch as he or she really is, with all the failings to which every human being is prone. The experience of the last few decades has amply shown that: in most cases where this happened, not least in marriages, some sort of disaster was the result. The success of a monarchy depends to a large extent on *not* bringing it to the people, but on keeping them as far away from the Royals as possible. In this way it does not really matter whether a king or a queen is intelligent, a nice person, doing a good job or the opposite. No-one outside the inner circle needs to know – ought to know. After all, it does not really affect the fate of the nation.

There can be no better example in recent history than that surrounding the unfortunate first marriage of Prince Charles. Without wishing in the least to go into the merits or demerits of the affair, basically what happened was that his marriage went wrong, he had a mistress and his wife had several lovers. So what else is new? No-one will ever know precisely in what order these events occurred; or ought to care. There are numerous examples of this in royal history without anybody having turned a hair. Look, again, at Henry VIII, who behaved in a rather less civilised fashion than Prince Charles. He, however, got all the stick, whereas the picture we have of Henry VIII is pretty well unscathed. The damage that resulted in the last few decades was to a large extent self-inflicted, by giving the public a ringside view. Of course, we lapped it all up, but paradoxical as it may sound, we secretly did not even *want* to know too much. Our resentment, so many of us say, was caused by the heir to the throne having to be a role model, and our condemnation of his adultery was based on that, no matter how we ourselves would or did behave in similar circumstances. I don't believe in that moral indignation. I maintain that the reason is largely subconscious, as it so often is: it threatened to affect our fairytale view of the monarchy itself. The proof? At the danger of repeating myself, the wish in some circles for Charles to resign. We knew too much about him. We preferred William, about whom we know literally nothing. Can we adduce any other remotely valid and reasonable explanation of our preference other than that, as far as the monarch is concerned, we prefer to adopt an ostrich attitude? Surely, it is further proof of the fact that the monarchy fills a need that defies explanation on other than a subconscious level. And the people's instinct is right; the institution does a lot of good for stability, whilst its built-in restraints ensure that it can do no real harm.

Could we think of anything with better qualifications? The people who tinker with it, should they, God forbid! ever be successful will probably not live to regret it themselves, but make no mistake, their descendants will.

*

5

Then and now

*"Not to be English was for my family so horrible a
handicap as almost to place the sufferer
in the permanent invalid class."*

Osbert Lancaster

This piece was written as one of the introductory sections of
my book "Where do you come from?"[19] It was intended to
show the first impressions we Jewish refugees received on
arrival in this country. To this extent, it can be called "semi-
autobiographical", but, additionally, it may be of interest to a
wider public anyway.

It is obvious that we refugees from Nazi Germany must,
both by assimilation and by passage of time, have become
very different people from those we were when we first
arrived in this country in the 1930s. But what is easily
forgotten is that, during that period, Great Britain itself
underwent very fundamental changes. The peaceful country
in which we found refuge almost two generations ago is in a
great many ways simply no longer comparable to what it has
become through social and other developments and
upheavals, many of which originated in, or were accelerated
by, the Second World War and its aftermath.

At the time it was an island in more senses that one. It
could be reached practically only by sea, something that
frequently meant a pretty uncomfortable and stressful
journey. This comparative isolation was undoubtedly one of
the reasons why it was so 'insular', so very different from the

---

[19] Pen Press Ltd.

Continental countries to which most of the British, with their nation still a world power, felt vastly superior. It was very rare for one of its citizens to talk it down, as happens so frequently today. As a result, we immigrants respected this attitude of superiority almost without question. This is to say, while we might have been critical of certain matters, customs and opinions, there were considerably more that impressed us greatly. I feel this country is likely to appear to any foreigner in a far less impressive light today than it did to us, to whom it was the 'promised land' which we had been very fortunate and relieved to be allowed to enter. This was bound to influence our general attitude. If the natives of a country are not critical of it, new arrivals are unlikely to find too many faults of their own accord. Strange customs – yes; open to strong criticism – normally no.

Some of the national characteristics immediately apparent to us were, for instance, the general courtesy – people colliding in the street, no matter which 'class' they belonged to, would both automatically say 'sorry' at the same moment, a habit so very different from the more common reaction we had been used to in our homeland. There, we would have been more likely to hear something like an angry 'Can't you look where you're going, you fool!'

We noticed the (today almost unimaginable) quiet atmosphere in restaurants as opposed to the noise in Continental establishments; the absence of pushing in a queue and, for that matter, the custom of automatically forming one. Speakers in Hyde Park with its often weird performers and good-natured audience, which normally required just one or two Policemen to curb any occasional over-enthusiasm, were a revelation, something that would have been unthinkable in most other countries. It was one of the sights of London we considered worth reporting in letters home. We marvelled at the London Bobbies, unarmed, friendly and helpful servants of the public, so very different from our perception of the German policeman, strictly a representative of public authority and showing it on every suitable or unsuitable occasion. We noted the full accessibility of Government quarters, including Downing Street – no barricades. Then there was the fact that many residents did not in the least worry about leaving their front doors unlocked, the risk of possible intruders simply not entering their heads. People of all ages and both sexes went out at night without giving a thought to possible muggers – and so on.

All this appeared to us far more important, and rightly so, than the occasional strange-seeming customs and attitudes. Those were the good old days, never, I fear, to return!

In view of the perceived vast superiority of the British over us, the idea that we ourselves might one day be able to contribute something of value did not occur to most of us unless we were one of the chosen few in the worlds of art and science, whose fame and reputation had preceded them and who were received with open arms, representing, as it were, a welcome by-product of the German persecution. They were accepted not with reluctance or condescension, but considered as actually worth competing for. These, though, were far from typical refugees. There was very little doubt that the modest opinion most of us had of ourselves was shared by our hosts. At that time the certainty that 'British is best' was well-nigh axiomatic. The British tendency for understatement definitely did not extend to the almost touching self-belief – or should I say self-deception? – expressed by prominent people and in the press.

Let me give a few examples.[20]

'We own the brightest posters and gayest underground station in Europe'. (*Star* 18.6.1920. At that time the word 'gay' did not, of course, have its present meaning.)

'I met a man yesterday who has travelled halfway across the world, to find that the greatest wonder of the world is – the Englishwoman! He is the Sultan of Zanzibar'. (*Sunday Express* 9/6/1929.)

'The most famous piece of statuary in the world... (is the)... fountain... surmounted by the statue of Eros in Piccadilly Circus'. (*Sunday Express* 20/10/1920.)

'England has more beautiful and valuable pictures than any other country in the world'. (*Evening Standard*

---

[20] I am taking them from a book by GJ Renier, published by Williams and Norgate Ltd in 1931 and re-published by Ernest Benn Ltd in 1956. Today it is out of print, largely forgotten and not easy to get hold of, but at the time it achieved no fewer that 14 reprints. This success may in part have been due to its very cheeky title: *The English, Are They Human?*, but there is no doubt that it offered a number of valuable insights into the English character and conditions of life at the time, as seen by a foreigner who was not a refugee but had chosen of his own free will to live and work in England. While, in my view, the author on occasion sounds somewhat ambivalent, the opinions he expresses are free from the inferiority complex so often experienced by the typical refugee whose self-esteem is affected by his precarious position. Thus it sometimes provides useful independent confirmation of our own opinions. I am sure that the author's choice of examples dating from 1926/30, thus a few years before the German refugee immigration began, is irrelevant, because there had been no perceptible change in British conditions during the intervening years.

Incidentally, the reaction to the book by the typical British citizen could be one of considerable annoyance. I remember recommending it in all innocence to a British lady as a good read. She never spoke to me again.

12/6/1920.) [21]

'The British Post Office is one of the few wonders of the world...' (Notes, Organ of Association of Head Postmasters, December 1929). Of course, to paraphrase Mandy Rice-Davis on a later occasion: 'They would say that, wouldn't they?'

'The British Press, taken as a whole, is the best, the fairest and the cleanest Press in the world'. (Stanley Baldwin 24/6/1930.)

'The best waiters in the world are the fully qualified English ones'. (*Evening Standard* 22/2/1930.)

'The middle-aged Englishman, travelled and moderately wealthy, is the greatest gourmet in the world, better even than the French'. (*Evening Standard* 19/3/1930.)

'British cooks are the best in Europe... We did not find an honest British bun anywhere in Europe... Greek and Viennese bakers were greatly impressed by the Eccles cakes, current buns and mince pies...' (Spokesman for the National Association of Master Bakers, Confectioners and caterers, 1929)

.

'Let us cure ourselves of the habit of pretending that the British climate is the worst in the world. In fact, it is the best in the world'. (*Sunday Express* 14/7/1929.)

Enough of that. I am not here to comment. My intention is to write about German and Austrian refugees, not British

---

[21]This is neatly matched by the opinion offered by the art critic and scholar John Hunt (1775-1849): 'Rembrant is not to be compared in the painting of character with our extraordinarily gifted, English artist, Mr Rippingille'. (The *Cassell Dictionary of Humorous Quotations 1999*)

social history. Some of the opinions quoted, whilst hardly defensible today, may have been more true 80 years ago. Whatever the case, they show a nation at that time unconditionally convinced of its superiority in practically everything, and not shy to express this opinion loudly, clearly and unambiguously as a self-evident truth. How else could *The Manchester Guardian* have written, on 16/1/1930: 'We are the most self-deprecating people on earth'. I can only assume that the author was a comparative newcomer to the world of journalism and not greatly interested in anything his colleagues had written, otherwise he could hardly have missed the examples I have just given.

Looking back, I cannot exactly remember how we reacted consciously to this constant refrain of self-congratulation; but subconsciously, since we were already conditioned to think extremely highly of England, we found little of it particularly questionable, except perhaps the remarks about the British climate and English cooking. Of course, most of us were not particularly avid newspaper readers at the time, but these opinions, constantly reiterated, were bound to be reflected in the attitude of the average British citizen. It is clear that this must have contributed to our strong subliminal conditioning and thereby have had a profound influence on our views.

Thus, if we talk about our early days, we have to remember that in a great many respects we spent them in what can almost be called a different country from present-day Britain, and with people vastly more self-confident and self-opinionated than they are today. It is an intriguing question whether we would have felt and fared markedly differently if conditions had been the same then as they are now. Well, we shall never know, though the attitude of many of today's immigrants does give an indication.

6

Old age

> *"Funny! Everybody wants to get old,*
> *but nobody wants to be old."*

Anon

John Mortimer, whose writings I greatly admire, has defined old age in his "Summer of a Dormouse" as the time at which a man is no longer able to put on his socks himself. I am older than he is and, at the time of writing this, can still (just) manage to perform this difficult feat. So there must be other criteria. But, apart from the number of years one has spent on this earth, it is not easy to find anything that necessarily has general validity. Aging can express itself in the most diverse forms. And it can be a very lonely business; everyone has to try and deal with it in his or her own way. I can do no more than speak for myself and, of course, only as a man.

One interesting feature is the attitude to the loss of sex drive. As I said just now, I can only speak from personal experience, but considering the importance of sex in the life of any normal man, I regard this loss as a less calamitous event (or should I say non-event) than I had anticipated. Just as most of us are not particularly interested in food if we don't feel hungry, so the concern with sex diminishes with the appetite for it. For this reason you may feel almost no actual deprivation. Naturally one looks back with nostalgia on one's former more or less happy memories (yes, even the less happy ones). The almost total absence of the suffering we may have experienced at the time, can be counted as one of the, oh so few, blessings of old age. In fact I have read about people who were glad to be rid of the scourge of sex; as for myself, I certainly would not go as far as that. Anyway, nostalgia is not painful. It is just, well, nostalgic.

But feeling little deprivation is not necessarily the general attitude. There is the feeling of loss and stress some people do experience at the very fact of waning potency as such, never mind how much they really need the sex itself. This can be very hurtful for those, to whom continued virility is essential for their male pride and self-esteem. They will therefore make every effort to keep on recreating the past, so as to show that they can still be attractive to the opposite sex and can still "perform"[22]. I quite agree, of course, that to remain active in later years, in whatever capacity, is a means of keeping young, or rather postponing the symptoms of the inevitable. But if you continue with something merely in order to prove to yourself and the world that you are still capable of doing it, i.e., if the challenge and the anxiety connected with it become stronger than the enjoyment itself, it is time to consider seriously whether you should not call a halt and hang up your condoms, if I may put it like that,. But again, one cannot generalise. Some people continue to enjoy a healthy virile sex life into ripe old age without having to worry about a thing. Good for them!

For the others, be it in sex or in sport, continuing strenuous effort, more or less undiminished into old age is not to be recommended. Far from keeping young, it can be a danger to health. This has nothing to do with keeping fit through exercise within your capabilities, even if you find this, as I do, boring and time wasting. But I have managed to discover an effective method of overcoming this feeling and to keep exercising: I reason that for every half hour I spend in this way, I probably prolong my life by six hours. Thus, far

---

[22]Personally I have always considered this expression as something of a misnomer. Perhaps it is because I am the son of a concert violinist but "performing" has always meant to me in the first place doing something in public and for the benefit of others rather than oneself – not something you think about in connection with the sex act, unless you happen to be an exhibitionist or a porn star.

from wasting my time, I am actually gaining some. Childish, but it works – assisted by the fact that I listen to the morning news at the same time. But this is by the way, and certainly not recommended for sex.

Sex should not be confused with another emotion: the comfort and intimacy of a long-standing relationship in which sex as such is no longer the main feature and for which therefore there is no age limit. One of the additional "bonuses" is, incidentally, at least in my personal experience, that a long relationship has the effect of obscuring the physical signs of old age in your partner; you retain to some extent the original youthful picture.

As regards second marriages by older people, there are so many potential motives for them – the number of variations and combinations is almost endless – that it is impossible to bring them on to a common denominator. There may be the genuine wish of two elderly people who have fallen in love, to enjoy each other's companionship and shared interests without emphasis on sex. It can, on the other hand, be a marriage of convenience for a variety of reasons: to overcome loneliness, for a man to have the comfort of an unpaid housekeeper, carer or nurse, for a woman because she genuinely needs to care for and look after someone, or to be secure financially, and so on. These marriages can be decidedly happy, but I have found that there is one factor that is inevitably lacking: the shared experience of two young people, usually with limited means and all the attendant difficulties, on the threshold of life, building up a family and striving for a successful career. I am convinced that in happy marriages between young people, this creates an unquestioning dependence on, and commitment to, each other, that is missing from most second marriages, where both partners have been living their own separate lives for many years and have become set in their ways and opinions.

In addition, the "for better or worse, in sickness and in health" bit should not be overlooked. It does not apply to young couples in the same way as to old ones. One way or another, the financial background is usually a settled one, so there are no surprises there. The health part, on the other hand, can take on a very different acute meaning and exert an adverse influence to which, I cannot help feeling, it is advisable for both partners to give more than passing consideration before taking the decisive step. If this sounds selfish, it is not meant that way, but since old people are usually widowed and have therefore gone through a traumatic time, both partners should at least spare a thought to the possibility that this aspect can become far more realistic and stressful than anticipated. I have a number of female friends of advanced age, for whom I feel great affection, and for whom, if they were ill or otherwise in trouble, I would do all I could. But the difference is that in marriage you *identify* with the partner, and this makes it a vastly different kettle of fish.

What about older men marrying younger – sometimes substantially younger – women? I have known a number of men who had done so and who assured me that, for them, this was the fountain of youth – the precise factor that kept them young. And what happened? In not a few cases they did not manage to reach real old age at all. This may, of course, have had any number of reasons, but one of them, I venture to suggest, could well have been stress: their concern whether they were still doing a good job – not only sexually, but also in their leisure activities notwithstanding the age disparity. Consequently many of them had become, as it were, simply too ambitious and, let us face it, had to be wary of rivals nearer the age of their spouse. Not a good recipe for happiness and peace of mind.

In sex, as we all know, it is essential that both partners are satisfied. Mature people give undoubtedly more attention to this than young ones, something that can to some extent compensate for waning powers. When we were young and inexperienced, the partner was not necessarily our priority – our own satisfaction came first. Of course, this can also be the case in old age, if you are selfish and/or very wealthy.

Again, it is impossible to generalise; an old man can be sexually very attractive to some women, not least as a father figure. Or the lady in question may just be a gold digger. You see in the tabloid press from time to time photos of very old millionaires, with one and a half feet in the grave, canoodling with very young and superficially glamorous women. I find these pictures little short of nauseating for the onlooker and highly undignified for the couple itself. Nobody looking at them could possibly form an opinion in the least flattering either. An unattractive old man marrying or bedding an attractive young woman ought to be as discreet as possible about it, so as if nothing else, to avoid inevitable ribald comment behind his back.[23]

As I said, all this does not mean that old/young marriages cannot be happy. However, for me personally there are two more factors that, I feel sure, would prevent me from taking such a step (as if any young woman would have me!): The first is the question of starting a family. Children like to conform, and I have known a number of cases in which a boy or girl was thoroughly ashamed of having a comparatively so very ancient father. Quite unwarranted, of course, but there it was. But such a reaction in children is not necessarily inevitable, whilst another development is much more likely: very young children can be and usually are extremely demanding, unreasonable and a thorough nuisance. They will not only be successful rivals for the wife's attention, but in

---

[23] I cannot forbear quoting another highly applicable old joke, unfortunately in German and, being a play on words, untranslatable. On the occasion of such an old/young marriage the question where the happy couple will be honeymooning, is answered by: "In USA, vielleicht Canada" (kann er da).

It also reminds me of the old joke of the two school mates who meet again after many years. One has a beautiful blonde on his arm whom he introduces as his fiancée. His friend takes him to one side: "Are you really going to marry this young girl?" "Yes, next week." "But surely, this is ridiculous. We went to school together, so I know your age. We are both 85…" "Psst, not so loud! She thinks I'm 90."

addition will get on their father's nerves in no time. I have seen couples where I had the distinctly uneasy feeling that the father, even if hardly past middle age, was sorely tempted to do a whining child serious harm. The futile ways in which he endeavoured to cover up this feeling would have been almost comic if it had not been so sad. Horses for courses. Little children are for young people. Old ones can rarely cope comfortably.

A further argument against an old/young marriage is based on the age disparity in a different way: however harmonious the marriage and genuine the wife's feelings, the discrepancy is bound to be present somewhere in her mind. In the normal course of events, the husband is naturally certain to die long before her, and she would be less than human were she not to give thought to the question of what she would then be doing with the large part of her life still before her. Of course, most wives in question would indignantly deny any such feelings. I do not doubt that some would do so quite honestly. But I feel certain that they must be deceiving themselves; their feelings may well have remained in the subconscious, but they are present all the same. For me as the older partner, it would be extremely counterproductive to be, from the outset, just an episode in my spouse's life and, I suspect, it would affect our relationship. No doubt selfish, but I should be surprised if I were the only one harbouring such thoughts.

There are, of course, the cases already indicated where the elderly husband simply marries in order to have a nurse on demand, who can't easily give notice or where he generally welcomes the assistance and support he receives from a younger wife. This is a good basis for a successful relationship as long as both parties are clear about the facts from the outset. Yet, it is not really a "marriage". However, in these cases the older man usually does not mind the situation caused by the age difference and is – or should be – caringly and actively concerned about the position of his partner after his death.

Enough of sex and marriage. There are many other matters that affect us in old age. One of them is the change of our attitudes generally. I am avoiding the expression "change of character", because I do not believe that character as such depends on age. Characteristic attributes simply become more marked. It is certainly not true that everybody mellows with age. On the contrary, not a few of us may become gruff, choleric, demanding, more selfish than before, intolerant of other people's opinions and of modern developments generally – in brief, we may conform to the picture of the typical blimp, mother-in-law or similar figure looked at with a mixture of dislike, condescension and amusement. Other agers may go in the opposite direction, become less concerned about general matters, more tolerant, friendly and appreciative, even apologetic. Do not be deceived, gentle reader. This is often by no means the result of attractive character traits, but of something quite different: on the one hand, increasing helplessness, which makes us more dependent on others, the need to be liked, or the need to conserve our strength and not to get excited about too many matters. And on the other hand a certain laziness as well as indifference to what will follow after us – be it nuclear war, terrorism, global warming or whatever. You have to possess a very marked social conscience to worry overmuch in old age about something that cannot possibly concern you personally. And perhaps the feeling that you have lived a normal life span, had your fill of difficulties and overcame them more or less successfully, so that not too much can happen to you any more, is also one of the very few consolations of old age offsetting the envy you might feel of people who are still young. The latter is, incidentally, an open question. We might often say, "I am glad to be old and not having to face the difficulties in store for humanity". But I wonder what is the dominant factor – subconscious envy of the young or conscious relief that their problems will not be ours. But some of us also tend to say the opposite, and I shall deal with this presently.

What about the approaching end of our life? My young grand-daughter, studying psychology, once had to write an essay about the older generation and misguidedly interviewed me, in spite of my denials, as an example of "successful aging". The day after the interview she rang me up: "Granpa, there is one thing I forgot to ask you; what do you think of dying?" "Not much", I replied truthfully. But it set me thinking; obviously, we are all condemned to death from the moment we are born. We are all afraid of death – why is it, then, that in old age the average person is no more concerned about this inevitable event than the young or middle-aged one? Clearly, part of the answer is that we are programmed not to worry overmuch about something too far ahead to be a realistic factor. Conversely one would expect older people to think more and more about death the more ancient they get and by and large, of course, this is the case. But surprisingly, as long as we remain in comparatively good health, it does not play as large a part in our thoughts as one might expect. Is there an explanation?

There are many clichés about aging, not all of them true. For instance, we often tend to say, "it is amazing how time flies so much more as you get older." I am not sure that this is really so. Time, on the contrary, can hang heavily on our hands. Of course, we know that we have very much less time ahead of us than younger people, but we tend to push this thought into the background: after all, our time of death is still indeterminate. This is actually not without a certain basis in fact: our life span lengthens the older we get: at birth, it is around 70 or so; when we have reached that age it could be 78, at 78, 85, and so on. In other words it is a case of Achilles and the tortoise –in theory Achilles never catches up; statistically we always have some time left, even when we have become centenarians. This is one of the factors that enable us, albeit to a limited extent, to cope with the matter.

Another thing is that we don't *see* ourselves as old; we don't notice it, never mind that we are looking at ourselves, as we do, in the mirror every day. What old man or woman has not, when seeing a recent snapshot, exclaimed; "Good God, is that me? I look terrible! "On the contrary", will be the almost inevitable answer – "I think it is a very good likeness and you look very nice in it." We just deceive ourselves, and it is probably a blessing that we do.

We sometimes say with a sigh – "how wonderful it would be, to be 30 (or 40, or 50) again." I have already suggested that we do not always mean it, just as we don't mean the opposite. Do we really desire to lengthen our life span and go again through the struggles, disappointments and heartaches we experienced when we were younger? I claim that we don't really know, because we cannot recreate the fact that we were better able to cope with them than we would be today.

In a way, some of us are proud to be old. If we say to a very old man, "You look marvellous for an 80-year-old", he is not unlikely to reply something like, "I'd rather look less marvellous for a 60-year old." Here again, I often wonder whether he means it, whether a 20 years younger age full of ailments would really outweigh a healthy old age and, for that matter, the (entirely unjustified) pride in having achieved it[24].

A happy old age presupposes happy memories, and it is therefore important how we view our past. We should remember the positive events rather than the negative ones, and we should begin to forgive ourselves our past (past!) faults and mistakes. It is too late for guilt feelings. This at least is the theory – but as many of us will know, it is easier said than done.

The relationship with our descendants is another

---

[24] Not to mention the disagreeable old men or women – usually confined to novels – who, on opening the "Times" in the morning (they all read the "Times") first turn to the death announcements to find out whether any contemporary has predeceased them – and then gloat over it. Not what I would call a particularly attractive character trait, and one to which I can plead "not guilty" with a good conscience. And yet, and yet – could there be, subconsciously, something of that feeling in many of us? Carefully suppressed, of course, and entirely unacknowledged.

problem besetting us oldies. But can one really say anything about it that is universally true? After all, people's relationship with their children and grandchildren can vary from very close and loving to hostility; bitterness or disappointment, from dependence to independence; with 57 varieties in between, especially when, to coin a phrase, Mammon rears its ugly head. Yet I believe that, here, too, are a few points that may have some general validity.

For instance, I believe – disregarding possible financial factors of one kind or another – that the older party is as a rule the weaker one. With age, our physical and mental powers diminish, our social circle contracts; we no longer have an active professional life and through all this have become automatically less important and influential than we once were. Similarly most developments in technology and culture leave us standing. Who among us really likes, let alone understands, contemporary art and music? Who of us oldies can claim to understand, and therefore sensibly discuss, half of today's adverts on TV, either because we fail to see how they should make a certain article or service desirable, or even because we have no idea what in fact the ad is trying to sell? Yet they must be working for the generation for whom they are intended, or else advertisers would soon stop wasting their money.

The age gap between us and our nearest and dearest of the next generation(s) works in most cases to our disadvantage. How often do our children or grandchildren ask us for advice, and in the rare cases when they do, take it? And why should they? How often did we listen to our own parents with their out-dated views? By the same token, how often are we invited by our children to parties in which they entertain their friends of the same age? Again, for that matter, how often do we invite them to ours without being concerned that they might be a nuisance – "younger people talk much faster and less distinctly than formerly" – or, equally important, be bored? Let us face it, however good the relationship, our impact on the lives of our children, unless, of course, they have physically to look after us (or v.v.) or they are financially dependent on us, is very small indeed. The stories of domineering fathers, mothers, mothers-in-law and family patriarchs interfering in marriages, education, the kitchen or whatever are in my opinion largely mythical, unless the matter has other subconscious motivations not affected by the age difference – for instance the husband is a wimp.

If, then, our children are so much stronger, should this subdue us? Stop us from saying what we think? There are parents who consider it wrong in principle to express their opinions. I can't agree. But there is a big difference between expressing an opinion and nagging. When, as happens in 9 out of 10 cases, no notice whatever is taken of what I say or advise, I leave it at that. Repetition will make no difference. And who knows, I may in fact be entirely out of touch with present-day conditions.

We love to see our children and grandchildren, but should we complain if they do not visit us as often as we should like? Not if we want to prevent them from regarding visiting us as a chore. We want to show them, of course, that they are always welcome, but it is for them to take the initiative; it is the only way to make it as certain a possible that they really enjoy our company. And incidentally, I have not infrequently heard grandparents say of their young grandchildren: "I am very glad when they come to see me, but I am also not exactly sorry when they leave". Nothing wrong with that. It is a fact that, as we grow older, we lose flexibility and find it more difficult to cope with young minds.

It is different, of course, if we need their help in anything. In most cases this will be given without question. If it is not, it is time for us to ask ourselves whether the fault lies with us or with them.

I have always found that being too close, living as it were in one another's pockets, might give rise to unnecessary friction. And do not let us overestimate the effect of closeness anyway. I am reminded of the (true) story of a little girl, aged

9, whose grandmother (to whom she had been particularly attached) died during the night. Her parents decided not to tell her this upsetting news in the morning, but to wait till she came home from school. When they did, she burst into tears of genuine sorrow. And then she said: "Why didn't you tell me this morning? I might have got over it by now!" Yet I am sure that the closeness had been genuine. It was just the concept of it that was different. It says something about the way in which the younger generation think about our death. For them it is natural that we should go long before them (and indeed, few things can be worse than the reverse). To put it crudely, it is our place in the scheme of things to die first. We might as well reconcile ourselves to it.

Family relationships can be very complicated and sometimes difficult, but it is for us, the older generation, to work at them and make them as smooth and pleasant as possible –simply because they are more important to us than to our children. For us, our descendants are, in a way, the crowning of our lives; for them we are a chapter – important, but bound to close one day.

It is often said that childhood and puberty are the most enjoyable/stressful/happiest/difficult periods – take your pick – in a person's life. I think old age is not far behind.

*

7

How to complain successfully without really trying

Leverage!

It is frequently being said that the British, as a people, do not complain often enough. I am not certain that this is really true. At any rate I did not gain that impression in my profession as an insurance broker; but perhaps insurance is atypical in that it is a subject triggering off all sorts of strong emotions in policyholders, especially when they have to make a claim. Of course, there are born complainants who not only enjoy the process itself, but also retelling their successful or unsuccessful efforts. On the other hand, many of us like to avoid it, because it can mean a great deal of aggravation, frustration and trouble, not good for us, especially as we get older. This means that we sometimes allow people to get away with something that is crying out to be rectified.

Quite a number of articles and even books have been written on the subject. Frankly, I don't know how useful they are, for I have developed my own method, which hardly ever lets me down and, in addition, is quite pleasant to use. If there were a way of copyrighting or even patenting it, I would have done so long ago. But since there isn't, and the method seems to be largely unknown, I am offering it to my readers free of charge other than the price of this book. One successful application of my method will mean that you will have had your money's worth. How many books are there about which that can be said?

The name of the game is "applied psychology".

In my view, there are three factors needed for a complaint to be called both reasonable and successful.

It has to be about a matter that is (a) not too insignificant and (b) can be put right by the "complainee" or his superiors. If we encounter a rude employee in a supermarket and write a strong letter to the manager, we may get a note of apology, more likely than not run off on the computer, but there is nothing else we can expect. In a way, of course, our complaint has been "successful", since we were able to voice our indignation in no uncertain terms and thereby get it off our chest; but this is not the type of success I am referring to.

There must be as little effort and aggravation on our part as possible; and we don't want to make an enemy of the person whom we are complaining about – after all, we may have to deal with him or her on a future occasion, for instance if it concerns a bank employee.

It goes without saying that we must have a good case. If our complaint is unjustified or at least cannot be made to sound justified, even the most sophisticated method will be of no use.

Initially, of course, we will just be approaching the person who in our opinion is at fault. Often that is all we need to do – he or she will realise their mistake and put matters right without further ado. But if we don't get anywhere, and two letters or telephone conversations should normally be sufficient to establish this, we proceed to phase 2: we write a letter to the person's superior, preferably in fact the managing director and, if possible, addressing him or her by name; the switchboard of even the largest organisation will usually give it to us without trouble.

It is essential that in that letter we set out our case dispassionately, moderately, concisely and logically. Begin with an apology for troubling the top man with so trivial a matter, but you feel that he might be interested in a first-hand account of the manner in which the affairs of his company are being conducted. In suitable cases you could add that he might wish to know how the millions spent by his company on sophisticated advertising are being squandered when it comes to customer relations. He might wish to investigate whether his department is using the most modern methods available. But do not ask for the matter to be put right; just state your case.

By now you will no doubt be asking, "What else is new?" Wait for it!

You do not send off this letter. Instead you post-date it, normally by 5 days; by more only if it has to be sent abroad or there are holidays intervening.

You photocopy the letter and send the copy to the person whom you are complaining about, with the following covering letter:

"Strictly personal*!* (and don't forget to put this on the envelope, as well).

"Dear… (Sir, Madam, or name if you know it),

I enclose copy of a letter to…, which will be posted on the date stated. Since you may be asked to comment, I feel that in fairness to you I should give you advance notification.

Yours (whatever)…."

Do not deviate from this text. It is tried and tested. In particular no "unless", no remonstration and don't omit the "in fairness", which is in fact the key sentence. And, unless there are special factors, don't post-date by more than 5 days; it is just the right length of time – not too long, not too short.

And then sit back and wait.

Usually, you will not have to wait long: you have the recipient on the phone or a letter from him within a day or two, not infrequently thanking you for your fairness. But if you haven't, you will usually find that matters are put right in a miraculously rapid fashion.

If you think about it, the reason is obvious: the recipient sees – possibly for the first time – the case against him set out succinctly and convincingly; he recognises clearly that you mean business; he realises that – in an organisation of any size, anyway – he will be doing himself no favours by allowing this matter to go to higher authority or even to get into his personal file. At the same time he sees that you wish him no harm, and are in fact giving him every opportunity to put matters right without any loss of face. There can be no question as to what the reaction of any normal person will be. The main point is that of shocking him into the recognition of his fault and the possible consequences.

Your attitude towards the repentant sinner must be equally friendly in response to any approach. No reproaches or going over past ground; after all, you have achieved what you set out to do, and there is no reason why you should antagonise the person who has come to heel, and thereby risk undoing the good work.

What if you receive no reply within the 5 days? Well, on the date stated you simply send off the original letter to the managing director (or whomever) with a *handwritten* PS; "For your information, I gave Mr/Ms ... advance notice of this letter, but received no acknowledgement." If, after this, you still get no reaction, I am afraid this method has failed. But I can give you the assurance, that this is an absolute exception. And, after all, if it has been unsuccessful, no harm has been done and you still have all the other options open to you.

I myself have used this method often (banks, building societies, large retail chains, Lloyd's, to name but a few), derived a certain pleasure from it – a rare thing in complaining – and cannot offhand remember any failure. Friends, to whom I suggested it, were usually equally successful, but admittedly there were occasional hitches. An acquaintance of mine was troubled by the employee of a foreign embassy who lived in the flat next to him: his children were so noisy that it seriously interfered with his comfort, and the parents had done nothing in spite of many complaints. I advised him to write a letter to the ambassador with advance copy to the neighbour. This he did, but the neighbour rang him up next day with the words: "You probably don't realise it, but I am the man who opens all the letters to the ambassador." But he offered to put matters right, and did. Thus, the letter had been successful, albeit not in the way the writer had expected. In another case I advised an elderly lady who had a complaint to find out the name of the managing director of the company in question; I would write the letter in her name. She got the name, but was telephoned by the company on receipt of my letter; there was no MD of that name in the organisation! But in that instance, too, the matter was put right.

You can even use the method when you have no real complaint, but only a general grievance. My most successful example: for years I had applied for tickets for a very popular Opera Festival, but always unsuccessfully; no wonder, since there are regularly a great many more applications than seats. After 5 years of refusals I wrote a letter to the managing director, saying that I fully appreciated the position, but that this, after all, was not a lottery and notice should be taken of the number of years regular applicants had been unsuccessful. I added the phrase I have already recommended: "It seems to me that the people in charge may not be fully conversant with modern methods". Advance copy as usual to the box office manager. I received a phone call from him next day and got what I wanted; and rightly so.

And last but not least – let me repeat that this way of complaining does not cause you any aggravation whatever, but on the contrary a certain amount of quiet amusement and satisfaction in observing the effect of this softly-softly approach.

Good luck!

8

Kurt Hahn and Salem, his first Gordonstoun.

*"Education is what is left when you have
forgotten all you have ever learned."*

Anon

Strictly speaking, I suppose, Kurt Hahn belongs into section 2
"Who is not Who", in which I describe various people I have
met. However, as I also shall be dealing with his German
school, the precursor to Gordonstoun – Prince Philip was a
pupil at both schools – I felt that it warranted a separate
description.

The school's full name was (and still is) "Schule Schloss
Salem", Salem for short, situated in South Germany near
Lake Constance. Its premises – originally a monastery with
all the trimmings – are part of a castle complex belonging to
Prince Max von Baden. Until the 1918 German revolution
Prince Max had been the hereditary head of the Land Baden.
Towards the end of that war the German High Command
needed a sacrificial lamb that would admit to Germany's
defeat and ask the Allies for an armistice. They persuaded the
Prince to become prime minister and to shoulder this
distasteful burden. No wonder that he became a hate figure
for the radical Right who clung to the myth of Germany
having lost the war solely through treachery, the so-called
"Dolchstoß Legende".

Hahn had been the Prince's private secretary and
founded the school after the war. It was based on his
educational principles which were in the main a somewhat
curious mixture of Plato's teachings and British public school
traditions. Prince Max offered him the use of part of his castle
on very advantageous terms (if not in fact for nothing), an

illustration of the persuasive influence Hahn was able to exert on other people. He was indeed a towering personality who had an enormous, almost Svengali-like effect on most of his pupils. I have always maintained that, if he had asked us to jump from a second floor window into the street below, we would, I can only hope, have refused, but very likely only after having given the proposition serious consideration. He was, to my knowledge, not a fully-trained educationalist, but a man full of ideas and with a gift of putting them into practice – or rather, possibly, of finding people willing and able to do so for him; he himself was not a man willing to deal with too much detail. With hindsight, I regard him as an outstandingly brilliant amateur with all the good and bad points this entails. .

His outward appearance was equally impressive, not least because, if there was the slightest sign of sunshine, he wore a tropical helmet. This was not done for effect, but was necessitated by the fact that he had to be very careful: as a young man, he had had a brain tumour which had been successfully removed – one of the reasons why he held the medical profession in the highest esteem and suggested to many of his favourite pupils that they should become doctors.

The school was co-educational and undoubtedly one of the foremost and most progressive boarding schools in Germany. Some people held against it that it was too "Prussian" (or "Spartan", which to them apparently amounted to the same thing) but this was simply not true. The dorms were quite comfortable. Sport and physical exercise did play an important, but by no means decisive part. Admittedly, the day began, before breakfast, with a jog in which the whole school took part, but it was of no more than 5 minutes' duration, and once you had got used to it, entailed no special effort. It is also a fact that we had to take two cold showers a day, but this was not regarded by us as a hardship even in winter (though I shudder to think of it now) and had, as I shall explain later, basically quite different reasons. The school's scholastic qualifications were not outstanding, but by no means negligible. In 1928 when I did my A levels, we still had to take them at the state school in nearby Konstanz, but a few years later Salem gained the official right to hold them under its own steam.

To some extent the school encouraged self-government by its pupils: after a few years you had the chance and were expected, though admission was by no means automatic, to become a "colour bearer" and participate in the "colour bearing" assembly, which discussed and passed resolutions on a number of matters, but always subject to the school's approval. It reminds me a little of the well-known story of the wife who declares: "In our marriage, my husband decides on all important, and I on all unimportant matters. Important are questions such as the form of the next government, the justification of current or proposed legislation; taxation and similar weighty problems. Unimportant are, for instance, the choice of food and clothing, our budget, whom to invite to parties, when and where to go on holiday, etc." (A lesser-known, but to my mind better version is the husband saying: "In our marriage, my wife decides on the unimportant and I on the important matters; and my wife decides what is important and what is unimportant.")

One of the guiding principles in Salem was absolute honesty; nobody ever told a lie, cribbed or did anything similarly dishonest. Every pupil had a training plan and had to fill in daily whether he or she had done all it prescribed. If we hadn't, we were subject to certain disciplinary punishments. Nobody cheated. I can testify to the fact that this really works: on my first day at the school, I answered a question by reading it off a textbook I held on my knees. As it happened, I did so very clumsily and expected to be discovered and severely reprimanded, but nobody said a word; it was so unheard-of that it was simply not noticed. I realised from that day onwards, that lying was simply not on and I can say with a good conscience that I never consciously told an untruth during my whole stay at the school thereafter. If nobody else lies, you don't either, and v.v. – it is as simple as that. Whether this is a good preparation for real life, is another matter. Many years later, a subsequent headmaster of Salem agreed with me that it was not and represented a conundrum difficult to resolve.

A second important point was Hahn's almost panic fear of homosexuality, confirmed to me by a Salem teacher after I had left school. I think it more than likely – though I have, of course, no proof whatsoever – that he himself was a latent homosexual, but without question never a practising one. This fear was probably one of the main reasons for the school being co-educational as well as for the afore-mentioned two showers a day. But it went further than that: boys were not allowed to touch each other, whether in the most innocent friendly way or in anger. It was called "being sticky" ("kleben") an expression that had an intentionally unpleasant connotation. If you wanted to fight, you had to challenge the other boy to a boxing match over three half- minute rounds with very well-padded gloves, which was held under Hahn's personal supervision. Boxing against a stronger boy was sometimes used as a punishment. To me, this always seemed to be of doubtful value, but since there was no corporal punishment whatever, it was obviously a substitute, and the underlying idea was no doubt to provide the punished boy with at least the chance of defending himself and giving as good as he got. During my stay at the school I boxed three times and came to the conclusion that this was not a profession I was cut out for. I won only one of my bouts, though that against a boy who subsequently became a world-renowned atomic physicist. Few professional boxers can make a similar claim.

Another consequence of Hahn's abhorrence of homosexuality was the fact that the main school sport was not football or rugger, but hockey (and a little cricket) , since this gave the least chance of any direct physical contact with the opponent.

I cannot say whether acts of homosexuality between pupils occurred all the same, but I certainly never saw or heard of, let alone experienced, one. So much so, that I left school at almost 18 years of age without knowing what homosexuality actually was. I should think quite a record for a boy at a boarding school. And I was not the only one. When, shortly after leaving school, I visited a former class-mate, who incidentally had been much sought-after by girls at the school, we heard that a boy had been expelled on account of a homosexual act. Unbelievable though it may sound, neither of us knew what that meant and, what is more, was not ashamed to admit it.(Incidentally, I met the expelled boy many decades later; he had become a very upright citizen, a high-up mason, and certainly did not look queer to me).

At the same time I have to say that whilst the fact of the school being co-educational, may or may not have prevented homosexuality, it was quite counter-productive for another reason. There were of course, friendships between boys and girls, but they never extended to any near-sexual activity, even such as kissing. There may have been exceptions, of which I, in my innocence, knew nothing, but I am certain that the discovery of any such thing would have caused almost a sensation at the school. And no wonder. In the sexual culture of the mid-twenties of the last century, girls had to be strictly protected for co-education to be viable. This meant, that at least in Salem, the girls were surrounded by the invisible barrier of an absolute taboo, which made them unattainable in actual fact as well as in the minds of the boys.

This, again, was anything but a good preparation for life. When, about 10 years on, I happened to meet up with a group of four Old-Salem class-mates, I realised that, all of them, were in their second marriages, the first ones obviously having gone wrong in some way. This could not have been accidental, but had to prove something. I was the only exception, more by luck (and an outstanding wife) than judgement.

Every Salem pupil had a "mentor", one of the teachers, to help him in any difficulties. I can't remember having made any use of mine, and, in particular, sex was never discussed.

This left you without adequate knowledge of sexual matters, such as wet dreams, – another failing.

In my experience (I gather from the memoirs of some prominent Old Salemers that this was not everybody's opinion) race, religion, position and wealth of parents, etc. made no difference. The son of the impecunious village schoolteacher had the same standing vis-à-vis the school management and his peers as had the offspring of a famous writer, statesman or titled person. Everybody was judged on his or her own merits. I was probably particularly unobservant, but it took the whole first term for me to realise that one boy in the 6th form called Berthold, was in fact the son and heir of Prince Max. He received no different treatment nor did he expect any. I have sometimes wondered whether this might not have been the reason why our own Prince of Wales, who, at the instigation of his father, went to Gordonstoun (the school Kurt Hahn founded in Scotland after his emigration from Germany), disliked it so much. In this (as in many other respects) he differs from Prince Philip, who was very happy both at Salem and Gordonstoun. Of him Hahn once remarked memorably "His best is very good, his second-best is not good enough". Hahn must have had quite an influence on the young Philip: in public speeches he made for some years after his marriage to Princess Elisabeth, cognoscenti could discover not only ideas, but actual idiomatic expressions obviously emanating from his former headmaster. In course of time this wore off.

I have come to the conclusion that Hahn's judgement of people and some of his methods were sometimes questionable. Many of his blue-eyed boys, who achieved the position of head or sub-head boy at the school, amounted to comparatively little in later life, and vice versa. And as concerns his day-to-day decisions, I remember one boy in my form, a very intelligent, nice and harmless fellow, who suddenly disappeared, being kept incommunicado and sent home next day. He had turned out to be a kleptomaniac. No attempt at educational remedies or psychological treatment was made – he was simply eliminated. Many years later he committed suicide. This was of course not due to his expulsion at the time, but yet, I feel, to missed educational opportunities: how much might not have been achieved by the right methods?

Hahn was Jewish, yet by inclination a strong German nationalist, which at the time was no contradiction whatever. But curiously enough, it took him quite some time before he was able to convince himself of the fact that the National Socialists were evil. When he did, he showed commendable courage, advising, as far as I remember, Old Salemers that joining the SA was not compatible with Salem principles. After the Nazis came to power, he was promptly arrested, but subsequently released, probably on the intervention of influential English friends; at that time the Nazis were still anxious to create a good impression abroad.

On balance, I am glad to have been a pupil at Salem under Kurt Hahn as headmaster, so much so that I sent my own son to Gordonstoun at a time when Hahn was still in full charge. Since emigration from Germany, he had converted to Christianity, and whilst, in my family, we were not at all religious, my wife suddenly declared: "I am not going to send my son to a school whose headmaster has converted, probably for reasons of practical advantage. Ask him why he did it." Considering Hahn's overwhelming personality, this was anything but easy, but as a good husband and father, I did it. "Not for personal gain I assure you", he said. "But I am of the firm opinion that you can fight Communism only on a Christian basis." Right or not, this satisfied me and, more important, my wife, and my son spent a very useful and happy time at the school, excelling, unlike me, at every kind of sporting activity going.

Surprisingly, I read many years later, that for some time during World War II Hahn had been suspected by the British authorities of being a spy or fifth columnist. I felt so strongly about this, that I wrote a letter to the "Times" asserting that for a man like him, spying would have been an absolute impossibility.

The end of his life was not in keeping with his successes and to my knowledge not happy. While in New York in very hot weather, he experienced something akin to sunstroke with serious consequences, no doubt a remnant of his former brain tumour. He became temporarily deranged, soon fully recovered, but it left him with a more or less permanent depression. He was at the time still headmaster of Gordonstoun and, if what I have heard is true, was removed from his post by the school governors with unseemly haste instead of being allowed to retire gracefully. He spent his last years in retirement near his beloved Salem.

There can be no doubt that Kurt Hahn was, for all his shortcomings, a remarkable man and almost a legend in his own lifetime. His influence in his own field can be felt even today. I am glad to have known him.

9

Jewish Refugees: Language, humour, names and all that.

"Anglish is what we don't know."

Dorothy Fields.

This, too, was originally written for my book "Where do you come from?" dealing with the problems of Middle-European (mostly German) Jewish refugees from Nazi oppression. From the complimentary comments I received for that book, it became soon clear to me that for most readers this chapter had been the only one they had really delved into. I would have preferred a wider appreciation of my own ideas rather than the jokes, which, after all, were not my own. However, there it was, and since that book had been meant only for people interested in refugee questions, I felt that a wider public might equally enjoy this section. So, here it is "complete and unabridged".

I

You will recognise the German Jewish refugee not only by his accent, but also by certain mannerisms of speech. For instance, if you hear someone saying repeatedly 'Thank you so much', you can assume fairly safely that he was originally German. For some reason this particular phrase has impressed us deeply, probably because it is so entirely different from what is correct usage in German and is therefore regarded by us as particularly 'good English'. On the other hand, if someone asks us whether we would like, say, a second helping of something, and we would, we usually cannot bring ourselves to say a simple 'Thank you', because in German this can mean 'No'. And if the question happens to concern a liquid refreshment and we are asked, 'Would you like some more tea?', ten to one you won't hear us reply, 'Yes please, but only a drop'; it comes out as 'but only a bit' (ein bißchen', German for 'a little').

Generally, on the other hand, we like to anglicise even where this is unnecessary. For instance, the well-known pianist Natalia Karpf once told me that while British people would pronounce her first name correctly as 'Natalia', refugees would invariably persist in calling her 'Nataly'. Sometimes we take on the accent of that part of the country where we happen to live. I was amused by a client of mine, a factory owner who spoke English with a Berlin accent you could have cut with a knife, but who would invariably pronounce the word 'girl' as 'gel', something that was correct in the local dialect but sounded extremely strange when said by him. And generally there are a number of words whose correct pronunciation we find it very difficult to ascertain, partly because sometimes the natives differ themselves: 'dandelion', 'awry', 'subsidence' (this, incidentally, not even the BBC knows). Some can't pronounce the word 'misled' properly. And an acquaintance of mine was puzzled for a long time about what a 'milk pond' was (what was meant was 'mill pond'). Correct pronunciation is the main stumbling block. It reminds me of the story of the refugee who saw the newspaper headline of a review: 'Hamlet pronounced success'. This was the moment when he realised that he would never master the secrets of English pronunciation and started to learn Chinese instead.

You will sometimes recognise newly arrived refugees by their basically correct but rather old-fashioned language – 'descend', 'impose', 'implement' and so on. There was the 15-year-old refugee girl befriended by a British family who quarrelled with the son of her hosts and said to him haughtily, 'I shall have no more intercourse with you.' My own father, before his emigration, once wrote to a London friend asking him to contact me. He meant to say that I was staying at the same boarding house as a mutual acquaintance but it came out as 'My son Carl is living with Mr X.' It may have been my imagination, but I had the distinct impression of encountering some raised eyebrows next time I met my father's friend.

Generally, people are apt to give others' choice of words an unexpected sexual connotation. I shall not easily forget my embarrassed disappointment when, as a trainee with a firm of Lloyd's brokers, I showed my departmental manager a letter from the mother of a violinist, a child prodigy of some fame, whose violin I was being asked to insure. It was one of my first pieces of business and I was quite proud to have gained such a prominent client. But instead of words of encouragement I just received helpless laughter. The boy's mother, describing the violin, had written, 'My son has a very big instrument...' More serious, perhaps, was the story of a young girl who one afternoon visited the cinema by herself and had the ill-luck to find herself sitting next to an amorous neighbour who started fondling her knee. Horrified she exclaimed: 'Go on, go on!' I have no idea how the episode ended.

One divorced lady once complained bitterly about her husband who had suddenly left her after a 'ravenous marriage.' There is the story of another girl who, when asked by her office colleagues whether she had enjoyed a short leave of absence due to a family bereavement, replied, 'Surely not, as you can imagine: I was on passionate leave.' My little son was sorely puzzled when, on his 6th birthday, an old lady wished him 'many happy regrets.' This was somewhat similar to the refugee who, on taking leave from his hosts, said, 'Thank you very much for your hostility.'

Two stories which I am assured are true: one tells of a refugee who wanted to find a tea shop where he could have a cup of tea. He puzzled a passer-by with the question: 'Are there any Lyons around here?' The other is that of a Hungarian immigrant who wanted to ask the way from a gentleman who, try as he might, was quite unable to understand what was wanted of him. Being of a kind disposition, he eventually assumed that the man, who was pretty shabbily dressed, was begging and asked him, 'Are you hungry?' Highly pleased at having at last been able to get through, the Hungarian exclaimed, 'Yes, yes, I am!' 'Come with me,' the stranger said and took him to a restaurant where he ordered a sumptuous meal for him. 'Are you still hungry?' he asked at the end. 'Yes, I am!' It apparently took some time for the crossed lines to be disentangled.

Sometimes misunderstandings can be more embarrassing. There was a Jewish refugee couple, sincerely welcomed by the inhabitants of a small village. At Christmas they were invited to midnight carols and it was suggested to them that they should choose a hymn celebrating Christmas, something, I have to confess, that was by no means difficult for many German Jews. They knew precisely how to oblige their hosts with the right song: the German 'O Tannenbaum, o Tannenbaum, wie grün sind deine Blätter.' ('Oh Christmas tree, oh Christmas tree, how green are your leaves.') There was, as it turned out, just one snag, which must have had a somewhat dampening effect on the Christmas spirit: the tune of that song is the very same one performed enthusiastically by the British Labour Party at every meeting: 'The Red Flag'. Incidentally, in German there are a few less respectful versions of 'O Tannenbaum' and consequently no original refugee has ever been able to take 'The Red Flag' seriously after having heard it sung in Great Britain – once he had recovered from his surprise, that is.

Staying with the church, two eight-year-old boys, twins, who had come over with a Kindertransport, were fostered by a very nice couple in a village and received many small kindnesses and gifts from other villagers. Their foster parents were devout Christians who attended church every Sunday. So as not to leave the children unsupervised, they took them along. When the collecting plate went round and people dropped their pennies into it, the children, who had not understood a word of the service, came with compelling logic to the conclusion that these too were presents intended for them. So when the plate reached them, they tried to grab all the money in it. This, I gather, was their first and last church attendance. One can only hope that no-one in the congregation regarded this as proof of what they had doubtless often been told about the avarice of Jews.

The everyday matters of life were (and sometimes still are) equally full of pitfalls for us. What refugee in his early days could tell the difference between jam and marmalade, ham and bacon? Why did the British eat grass sandwiches (mustard and cress)? How could a father know that a kite he wanted to buy for his son's birthday was not called a 'dragon' in English as it is in German? The coal merchant who was asked by the lady of the house to deliver his load 'into my back passage' may have received the wrong impression of his customer – as may the firm with whom a refugee lady tried to discuss the repair of her 'shits'. When this had been cleared up, it turned out that the company in question were actually watch repairers whom the lady had mixed up with 'Wäsche' (linen) restorers. And the British family who had provided a home for a refugee boy considered him to be of subnormal intelligence when he simply could not understand why they wanted him to buy vinegar – 'Vinegar of what?' 'Just vinegar' – until it turned out that what he understood was 'weniger', which means 'less' in German.

One Austrian lady went into several kitchen shops trying to buy a 'creator'. She was unable to understand why the British did not know of the existence of such an everyday implement. Eventually the riddle was solved. What she had wanted to buy was a ladle, which in her home country is called a 'Schoepfer'. But the German dictionary she consulted was not aware of this particular meaning of the word. It had only the customary translation of 'Schoepfer': the 'creator' of the world – God. Other difficulties were more easily cleared up. One lady had forgotten the word for 'chicken', but was able to make herself correctly understood by describing it as 'the bird who lays eggs'. Another asked for 'dukes eggs'. Sometimes mistakes can be immediately deciphered by fellow refugees, like that of the man who told his friend that

113

he had had his 'blind gut' removed – the literal German translation of appendix.

On occasions, of course, the boot is on the other foot and it is the British who make linguistic bloomers in German – as did a man I know who visited a German town. Being a collector of toy pistols, he went into a shop first thing and bought two of the German versions. Returning to his hotel, he was anxious to try them out without delay but in order not to disturb his neighbours, he decided to muffle the sound with his bed cover. The inevitable result was, of course, massive scorching. Being an honest man, he went down to reception and reported the mishap to the shocked consternation of the receptionist at the desk: 'Ich habe in mein Bett geschossen.' (The only meaning this could have for a German was "I have shat in my bed!")

II

Understandably, refugee jokes are in the main about language difficulties, changes of name and similar matters. The point of these tales is that the perpetrator is not supposed to realise that he is saying or doing anything peculiar. Thus, he is apt to become an involuntary figure of fun, possibly even of pity. However, as far as refugee – or for that matter most Jewish – jokes are concerned, I maintain that this is usually far from true. I feel certain that most of these stories, and in particular those concerning our linguistic failings, were either deliberately invented by refugees themselves or, as far as they were involuntarily perpetrated, gleefully spread by them. This was one of the ways in which we were able to try and come to terms with some of the difficulties of our situation. And how else could these stories have been put about? Certainly not via non-German speaking people, who would not even be able to see the point of most of them.

Whether I am right or not, we refugees were (and are, as I have already shown) certainly not alone in committing linguistic boobs. A nation whose Government spokesman, on being asked in the House of Commons about the Prime Minister's plans for the rest of the day, can reply, 'This afternoon Mrs Thatcher is making herself available to Mr Gorbachev' certainly does not have the right to laugh 'at', only 'with' us.

When I first considered whether I should devote a section of this book to refugee jokes, I wondered whether it might be a waste of time. Refugees have heard and retold them so often that they are not just 'old' but 'ancient' hat. Was there really any point in dusting them off yet again? However, on reflection I realised that 60 to 70 years have passed since the 1930s and early 1940s, i.e. not just one but almost two generations. As you get older you tend to overlook the passing of time. I realised this only too clearly when I recently met someone who quite obviously was not yet in his fifties, and asked him unthinkingly what he had been doing during the war, completely overlooking the fact that he had not yet been born at that time. This sort of thing is probably one of the reasons why younger people so often no longer take us oldies seriously. On the other hand, stories that are 65 plus years old may be new for many people today. Anyway, don't we always say that the old jokes are the best? Of course, my fund of stories is limited and consequently I wrote a letter to *AJR Information*, the official German Jewish refugee paper, asking readers for help. I was overwhelmed with replies from many kind people. It was interesting to note, incidentally, that amongst many others, one or two stories were quoted in almost every reply.

Language jokes, though, often present yet another difficulty: most of them are plays on words which can be appreciated only by people who speak the foreign language in question, in our case German. Non-German speakers will not understand them spontaneously. Having to explain a joke is, as we all know, giving it the kiss of death. Nevertheless, I decided that explanations, where necessary for understanding, were the lesser of two evils. I first considered relegating them to footnotes so that German-speaking readers would not have to bother looking at them, but I found this made reading far less convenient. I hope my German-speaking readers will bear with me. So here goes, with a few examples. It is not always possible to be certain about their 'pedigree'; a few may not even have originated with refugees at all. But if they didn't they should have done.

To start with a few chestnuts (I forbear to repeat the daddy of them all, ascribed, I believe, to the first German post-war President: 'Equal goes it loose' a literal translation from the German for 'it [whatever the event was] will start any minute'):

On a crowded bus a refugee couple get separated, the wife finding a seat on the lower, the husband on the upper deck. When the conductor comes to collect the fare, the wife, who has no money on her, tries to indicate that her husband will settle it. But the way she puts it is liable to be misunderstood: 'The Lord is above, he will pay'.

A customer in a bakery observes another woman, somewhat heavily made-up; selecting a cake which she considers would be a suitable purchase for her too. She turns to the shopkeeper with the words: 'Can I become a tart like this?' (the only German meaning of tart – 'Torte' – is 'cake'. 'Bekommen' in German means 'get'). There are several versions of this joke, the best one, to my knowledge, with the baker replying: 'Too late, my dear, too late.' And there is another story (which I only mention for the sake of completeness, for every refugee knows it) with the same play on words. A woman at a greengrocer's, on being told the price of cauliflower, indignantly exclaims: 'Such much? I can become a cauliflower round the corner for sixpence. Behold it.' ('Behalten' is 'to keep' in German.)

A refugee complaining to his boarding-house proprietor: 'Expensive landlady! There is a train in my room and the ceiling is too short. If things don't improve, I shall have no election but to undress.' (All words have double meanings. 'Expensive' = the German 'teuer' = 'dear': the word for 'train' can also mean 'draught'; 'ceiling' = the German 'Decke', which can also mean blanket; 'election = 'Wahl' which in German also means 'choice'; and 'undress' in German is 'ausziehen', which can also mean 'move'.) I should perhaps add that in pre-war days the antiquated British heating and ventilation systems were a constant wonder to foreigners. Possibly on account of the prevalence of open fireplaces, draughty rooms were one of the main reasons for complaints by people arriving from abroad, whereas the British did not seem to mind them at all. There is no precise English expression for the all-embracing German word 'gemütlich' – 'comfortable' 'cosy' etc do not entirely fit. Someone suggested 'draughty' as the most suitable equivalent.

Another refugee has rented a room in a private flat. Late at night the telephone rings. The landlord is out, so the tenant answers it but cannot understand what is being said. In his frustration he shouts, 'Vy must you rink now? It is midnight and I am only a ghost here' (Confusion with 'guest'). He was no doubt the same man whose rent included 'lightning'.

- Probably the same refugee again, alone in the flat, this time during the day, answers the door to the gas man who says, 'I've come to see the meter.'

'I am the Mieter. Vat do you vant?' ('Mieter', pronounced 'meeter' in German, means 'tenant').

An extended version is the gas man replying, 'No, you are not', to which the tenant answers 'Yes, but I am the untermieter (subtenant)'

- A tourist arriving in Hawaii asks a stranger, who happened to be probably the only refugee who originally made it to Hawaii: 'Excuse me, can you tell me, do you pronounce this place Hawaii or Havaii?'

'Havaii.'

'I see, thank you very much!'

'You're velcome.'

- A woman goes into a chemist shop wanting to buy paper. 'Paper?' I am afraid we don't sell paper.'

'Yes, you do, it is the paper – ah – ah – for the smallest room.'

'Oh, you mean toilet paper?'

'Yes.'

The transaction having been successfully completed, the chemist asks 'Is there anything else you would like?'

'Yes, some soap, please.'

'Toilet soap?'

'No, for the face.'

This, presumably, is not a true story, and brings me to the large number of jokes and anecdotes that have entered refugee lore.

- In the early days, marriages between female refugees and Englishmen were a rarity and, it must be admitted, sometimes probably marriages of convenience from the lady's point of view. In one such case the bride, on being asked at the marriage ceremony to repeat 'I shall obey my lawful husband', is said to have repeated it in the best Freudian tradition as 'I shall enjoy my awful husband'. Hopefully she was not the same lady about whom it was said later, 'Her marriage has not been consumed.'

- During the early years of the last war the official bulletins unfortunately had to report a string of disasters for the British. Two refugees are discussing the situation: 'Can you understand these reports?'

'Oh yes, quite well. Only one thing puzzles me: who is this General Wit-h-Drawal who is being mentioned so frequently?

- A written invitation ends with the words 'Don't dress as we shall be intimate.' (A literal translation with a nice double entendre. In Germany, in the olden days, 'to dress' meant to dress formally. The word 'intim' had no sexual connotation. 'Im intimen Kreise' simply meant 'amongst good friends', 'informal dress'.)

- On a wedding invitation the recipient, a refugee, is puzzled by the footnote 'RSVP' and asks a friend that he thinks it means, 'Quite simple: Remember se veddink present.'

- An immigrant, being asked at the customs whether his luggage contains any pornographic material, replies: 'No. I don't even possess a pornograph.'

- A recently arrived refugee at a bus stop: 'I know myself not out. Must I stand snake?' (Literal translation of the German grammatical structure, plus that in German to 'stand snake' means 'to queue'. 'Schlange' means 'snake', hence 'Schlangestehen' in German.)

- Board meeting of a company whose directors are all refugees. The firm's accountant asks: 'Who is chairman?'
'We all are, but we are naturalised British.' (The way refugees mispronounce the word 'German' is notorious).

- 'Nice day today, isn't it?' does not exist in German as a greeting. (Nor does it, for that matter, in the USA, where on one occasion I was almost physically attacked for uttering this sentence to a New York lift attendant who believed I was trying to wind him up). We refugees have learnt to understand the meaning of this phrase, but not necessarily that of its follow-up, 'Spring in the air!' to which one refugee is said to have replied, 'Vy should I?' ('Spring' in German is 'jump'.)

- A German Jewish couple at a grocery shop: 'We'd like some fruit drink.'

'Juice?'

Husband to wife: 'There you are, they are already starting here, too.'

- Friend to grandmother: 'Congratulations! I hear your grandson has been accepted for Oxford. What is he reading?'

'Oh, all sorts, *Gone with the wind, Suzy Wong...*'

- And so as not to forget the classical scene: someone was asked whether he knew the English for the first line of Hamlet's soliloquy, and proudly quoted it: 'His or not his, that is the question' (A re-translation from this excellent transposition into German, 'Sein oder nicht sein'; 'sein' has double meaning, 'to be' or 'his')

We develop after a time a mixture of languages of our own, which an imitation of 'Franglais' I might call 'Engman' or if you prefer, 'Gerlish'. Many of us amused ourselves with literal translations of British words and sayings or expressions such as 'I must schon say', (a plaintive mixture of German and English), 'guest giver' for 'Gastgeber' (host), 'Schweizer Häuschen' for London's Swiss Cottage, around which the bulk of refugees lived; 'one sausages oneself halt through' (again a mixture of the two languages, 'sausage through' being a verb for the German 'durchwurstein' = 'muddle through'.) 'This tie does not stand you' (the German verb 'stehen' can mean 'stand' or 'suit'). I cannot more, I break together' (a literal translation of the German 'I am at the end of my tether, I am having a breakdown'). Or, defensively about a woman who has become the object of malicious gossip: 'She is better than her cry.' (The German 'Ruf' may mean 'cry' or 'reputation'.) 'Gentlemen upon the ladies!' is the literal translation of an entirely proper German toast in honour of the female guests.

Some probably involuntary boobs were the way in which an employer dismissed an employee who would not mend his ways: 'I have told you once, I have told you twice – now it is so weit' ('now the time has come.') Or the waiter in a restaurant drawing a customer's attention to the fact that her scarf had fallen down: 'You dropped what.'

We also used literal translations of English expressions which could have a very strange sound in German – for instance 'Flaschenhals' for bottleneck. As someone said, bemoaning his somewhat haphazard use of the language: 'with mein English is it not so white hare' a homonym of the German 'nicht so weit her', meaning not much to write home about.)

There was of course, a non-linguistic kind of refugee humour too, though it was far less frequent. One of the nicest stories I remember is that of a refugee doctor who had just started his practice and was waiting for prospective patients to notice his existence. He wrote to a friend: 'Yesterday I had one patient. Today my consulting hours were a little quieter.'

Two friends meet. 'Have you got a job yet?' 'No, but I have hopes. Meanwhile I am polishing up my English'.

'Wouldn't it be better if you were to English up your Polish?'

The same friends are sitting on a bench in a park when a lark drops something on the head of one of them. Victim: 'And for the English he sings!'

III

Names presented problems in several ways. There were first of all those which were virtually 'impossible', such as 'Liachowsky', more than difficult to pronounce in English, let alone to remember; or those with a double meaning, such as 'Worms' (after an ancient and beautiful German town in which, inter alia, Martin Luther in 1521 defended his theses). Interestingly enough, though, I knew two refugees named Worms, both doctors who were sufficiently proud of their original name to keep it without alteration. I myself was, albeit not to the same degree, in a similar situation. English people would invariably spell my name 'Flesh', for which the

German word is Fleisch, and English Jews would occasionally pronounce my name in this way, apparently convinced that I had anglicised my name (which in fact derives from the German word 'Flasche', 'bottle'). 'Fleisch' does not always sound very attractive to German ears and therefore German refugees like to avoid saying it or even the English 'flesh'. Thus, a refugee lady, suddenly remembered that there was a member of the Flesch family among those present. In order not to sound offensive, she hastily referred to her offspring as 'my meat and blood'. Anyway, I kept my name and was pleased when my British-born children did the same.

But a great many people did anglicise their names or changed them altogether. I remember someone called Ellbogen (German for 'elbow') who did not translate it literally as he might have done, but quite cleverly changed its spelling so as to make it sound the same as before: 'Elboughan. In the same vein Hahn became Hawn and someone called Liebl (pronounced 'Leebl' in German) changed his name to Leigh-Bell. Rosenberg became Montrose, Schoenberg Beaumont. Another famous example was that of two brothers named Schwarzschild (Blackshield): One changed his name to Black, the other to Shield. Name changing became near-obligatory for all refugees who joined the army during the war, in particular the Pioneer Corps, without at that time having acquired British nationality. The idea was to give them some sort of protection in case they became prisoners of war and were executed by the Germans as spies. I have my doubts how much this would really have helped them, but fortunately, to my knowledge, the matter was not put to the test.

Some members of the army, as well as civilians, adopted, rather unjustifiably, very famous names such as Churchill, Nelson etc. For members of the Forces, the changes had to be approved by the commanding offer, and many got away with the near-blasphemous renaming. One man who was not so lucky was a soldier who wanted to call himself Clark Gable. He had some justification as his German name was Konrad Giebel (German for gable). Interesting that the name of a famous film star was more sacrosanct to the commanding officer than that of Nelson, a historical world figure. Adopting very English names did not always end well. Someone calling himself John Gay, for instance, may have come to regret it. Others had a certain amount of logic on their side. Someone over 6 ft tall called himself Longfellow. Braunberg became Browning, Schiller became Shelley etc. Someone with a good sense of the original called himself Anders (which in German simply means 'different'). Another, equally witty, called himself Werth. His original German name had been Wertheimer and, as he said, by dropping the 'eimer', he had 'kicked the bucket' (bucket = Eimer in German).

There was a story making the rounds about a refugee who changed his name to Shelter. The joke was that his previous name had been Liftschitz (which sounds Yiddish for the German word 'Luftschutz' = Air Raid Precaution). I believe there were none who got their names by accident, but during previous immigrations this was apparently more likely to happen. The story goes of one immigrant who, when asked for his name, replied in his mother tongue with 'schon vergessen' ('already forgotten') and ended up as 'Sean Ferguson'.

When you met a refugee with a very English and therefore obviously adopted name, you often played a mental game, trying to guess what he had been called originally. When eventually, rather tactlessly, you asked him whether your guess had been right, this could be embarrassing in cases where the person in question happened to be a British-born 'passport Englishman' and was resentful at having been mistaken for being non-British. Awkward situations in a different way could arise when the adopted name was a fairly common one and British-born people of the same name, on happening to hear it, asked its bearer which part of the family he belonged to. A friend of mine who had adopted the name

'Hilton' used to reply to this question, 'The Irish Hiltons.' He always got away with it. Some people were too proud or found it unnecessary to make a change. One of them was a friend of mine named Fuchs which in German is pronounced Fooks. When he became naturalised, he announced, 'Now that I am an Englishman, I want my name to be pronounced the English way – Fucks.' Someone had to tell him the facts of life.

The name game was not only played by individuals. There were also commercial firms with names they would probably have avoided had they been longer in this country. The name of one of my clients invariably caused some amusement in the firm of Lloyd's brokers with whom I was co-operating at the time, proving that no profession is free from people looking for the double entendre where none is needed. The company was called 'Ram Accessories'. But the best one, to my mind, was the name with which a firm manufacturing precision engineering parts chose to describe its activities: 'True Screws'.

Not that native Britishers did not make fun of us in turn. I remember during the war, a bus conductor on a route through Hampstead, the district where most refugees congregated, calling out 'Finchley Road' as 'Curfewstendam' (Kurfürstendamm had been pre-war Berlin's Oxford Street, and the play on the word 'curfew', to which we refugees were subject, was obviously irresistible). Along similar lines is the story of a woman who is sitting on a bus when the conductor, collecting fares, steps heavily on her toes. Startled, she exclaims 'Verbrenn!' ('May you burn', one of the many colourful Jewish curses uttered by people against those they are annoyed with but wish absolutely no harm in mind). The conductor replies: 'Change at Golders Green' (which is near the best-known London Crematorium).

Then there was the young Irish waitress employed in one of the restaurants mainly frequented by refugees, who claimed that she was quite unable to learn any foreign language. In spite of this handicap she had managed, through

124

constant repetition, to retain two German phrases which German visitors to the restaurant, mostly Berliners, invariably greeted each other with: 'Tach, wie gehts?' 'Danke, Beschissan' ('How do you do?' 'Thanks, shitty'). Part of the joke lay in the 'Tach', the very Berlinish abbreviation of 'Guten Tag' (good day).

Then there was the story of the bus load of refugees from Germany all being allocated to the same village until they could be dispersed. The reception committee was ready and did its best to make the arrivals welcome. One old man seemed particularly tired, staggering exhausted from the vehicle.

'You poor man, here, have a cup of tea. You must have had a terrible journey.'

'Yes, I'm afraid I did.'

'Where do you come from?'

'Dover. I am the driver.'

Yes, times were difficult for us, but not without their light relief.

10

The show must go on.

"Why must the show go on?"

Noel Coward.

When I wrote this piece for my book "And do you also play the violin?" I was thinking mainly of the acting and musical profession. But in the course of writing it I realised that the subject has a much wider application – in fact it concerns practically everybody. I feel therefore that it belongs in this collection.

'The Show Must Go on' – the Eleventh Commandment for actors, musicians, indeed, for all those who are in some way concerned with public performances. Everybody will do his or her utmost to avoid calling off a concert or show, even in the face of seemingly insurmountable obstacles – an admirable principle. In taking a closer look at it, I mean no disrespect. I would like just to give some thought to two questions. Might there be more to it than meets the eye? And has there been, during the past few decades, a trend towards watering down this attitude – 'dogma', rather – in some respects?

Let me say right away that this problem hardly ever arose in my own experience as far as it concerned my father. He was spared serious illness until shortly before his death. He sometimes suffered from bouts of sciatica and, on one such occasion in the United States, performed the Brahms Violin Concerto sitting down, at that time apparently an unusual feat which earned him, as he describes in his *Memoirs,* a hero's acclamation. What he does not mention in his book is another occasion when he came very near to cancelling a performance. I well remember the exact date – 8 October 1923 – because his fiftieth birthday fell on the following day – hardly a propitious time for a catastrophic public appearance.

He had arranged an orchestral concert jointly with a young conductor (his name does not matter) who was anxious to make his Berlin debut and was prepared to bear part of the expenses; considering the ruinous economic conditions following World War I, this suited my father very well. It seems that for this reason he had – untypical for him – not enquired very closely into the young artist's qualifications. No doubt he felt that anybody prepared to lay out a substantial amount for an orchestral concert would possess the appropriate technical and artistic equipment.

The programme contained two solo items, the Brahms Violin Concerto and the *Fantasie* by Josef Suk, a work my father liked enormously and played superbly well.

But the young man was anything but a good accompanist. This would not have mattered with the Brahms, where the Berlin Philharmonic could, if necessary, have followed my father without a conductor, especially since they had played it with him dozens of times in the past. But the Suk was different, because it was – and still is – performed only very rarely and the orchestral part is complicated.[25] The conductor simply could not master it.

My father became so worried that he seriously considered calling the concert off. This was not one of those situations, such as with illness, in which cancellation had become unavoidable, but one in which he had to decide whether to take the risk of damaging his professional reputation through no fault of his own. In the end the 'Show-Must-Go-On' axiom prevailed. The concert performance of

---

[25] As Suk himself acknowledges in a letter dated 18 May 1911: 'The Fantasie is not one of those solo works where one rehearsal is sufficient for conductor and orchestra, and the conductor has to be fully familiar with the score; but, of course, in this regard one can rely on Nikisch absolutely – others would have to be told beforehand'.

the Suk showed in places distinct 'Flesch improvisations' and cuts so as to avoid, as far as possible, parting with the orchestra. As he said afterwards, it had been one of the most nerve-wracking experiences of his concert career, earning him, incidentally, the undying admiration of the leader of the Berlin Philharmonic, Maurits van den Berg. Apart from my father, he was probably the only person in the hall who really knew what was going on; and this includes the conductor.

The reviews were favourable. One of them mentioned that the violinist had initially been playing in a somewhat 'carefully probing manner. 'The man doesn't know how right he is', was my father's laconic comment.

The 'Show-Must-Go-On' phenomenon has two aspects, one physical, one psychological. My knowledge of the first stems mainly from a very inartistic source – my professional activity as an insurance broker. In the course of my career I became, not surprisingly, something of a specialist in 'Non-appearance Insurance', as it is called in insurance jargon. To stop any misunderstandings, let me say right away that this is not a commercial. My work in the insurance field is now purely consultative, and arranging policies as such no longer forms any part of my activities. But the subject is both of interest and relevant in this context. I am restricting myself, incidentally, to 'serious' music, not pop, jazz and the like, where conditions are somewhat different.

Understandably, the musical profession and the insurance industry view the subject from two diametrically opposed angles: musicians claim that cancellations practically never happen; insurers take a more jaundiced view. To some extent both sides are right, because individual attitudes adopted by artists or promoters can be substantially different.

Most artists are extremely reliable and some promoters most helpful and inventive in order to avoid cancellations. It would be wrong to single out any one individual, but I cannot forbear from mentioning two names. The first is Daniel Barenboim who once, at a moment's notice, agreed to deputise for a colleague at an Edinburgh Festival concert, cut his finger while shaving and yet went on. Ever since I tried to negotiate reduced rates for him whenever I was asked to insure him (he does not know this; most insurances of this kind are taken out by promoters, not the artists themselves).

The second is the impresario Victor Hochhauser, who is uncannily successful in surmounting a crisis and keeping a show going. He certainly had to employ all his diplomatic skills then, many years ago; he managed to avoid the Bolshoi Ballet calling off a London appearance in the face of strong political agitation, culminating in throwing drawing pins and chasing mice onto the stage. Another achievement already mentioned elsewhere in this book was his obtaining permission to go ahead with a public performance of the Vienna Boys Choir.

At the other end of the scale are artists known to be so unreliable that insurance for them is obtainable only at near-prohibitive premiums, if at all. A marked proportion of these consist of singers of either sex whose vocal powers are on the wane. Obviously, I am not going to name names, except – and this for a special reason – that of Richard Tauber. In his case, non-appearance insurance was practically impossible, for as already stated elsewhere in this book he had once called off a sold-out Albert Hall matinee shortly before it was due to start.

What was apparently particularly held against Tauber was the fact that he was seen visiting a cinema the self-same evening. There is, of course, no reason why someone with a sore throat should not attend a film show; and television, at that time, was still a thing of the future. But one has to admit that the moment was not particularly well chosen.

Yet I remain convinced that his motivation for the cancellation was perfectly honest and genuine. He was the last person to let anyone down, be it public or promoter. Indeed, this was probably the key to his decision – he regarded a bad performance as one way of 'letting the audience down'. That he was a real trooper became clear to me during a matinee performance when I witnessed a basically unimportant yet quite significant example of the way in which he comported himself.

The concert took place at Queen's Hall in London – alas destroyed in the early days of the Blitz. I was listening from a small ante-room immediately behind the stage; all artists had to pass through it on their way to and from the platform. Those old enough to have been present at one of Tauber's performances will recall his exaggerated arm movements, a habit which I always found rather irritating – until the day of that concert.

At the end of his first number, Tauber walked off, as usual, in full flight, arms flailing. There were three steps leading down from the stage to the ante-room and when he reached them he *jumped* them. It was only then that I realised that he had one rather stiff leg and that all his movements, and of course the jump, were designed to divert attention from this disability.

Many people considered him conceited. Though he had every reason to be – some of his Mozart recordings are pretty well unsurpassed even today – he was not. He was easy-going and approachable if perhaps somewhat naively egocentric – a character trait he shared with many other artists. He once asked me to insure him against the risk of losing any piece of paper on which he might have sketched a tune that had just occurred to him. It is improbable that a Schubert or Mozart would have felt a similar necessity of protecting themselves against the loss of their inspirations, no doubt musically more valuable. The funny thing was that I did succeed in finding a Lloyd's Underwriter prepared to accept his proposal. At that time I was still very young and inexperienced; today I can only shudder at the thought of how I would have arrived at a satisfactory claim settlement if a loss had occurred; luckily it never did.

I cannot remember from my own experience any performance Tauber ever cancelled, although he made his last opera appearance – on the occasion of a visit to this country by the Vienna State Opera – when he was already terminally ill.

I value the memory of a great artist and a charming personality.

***

Now for the 'psychological aspects': for what reasons would a show normally *not* go on? Apart from genuine force majeure such as an earthquake or a fire destroying the concert hall, it would in the first place be illness or accident suffered by an indispensable member of the cast; or a performer's severe emotional upset caused, for instance, by the death of a close relative. In these cases, no one would normally expect a business or professional man to come to work. Either a colleague will stand in for him, or it just has to wait; it must be something of quite outstanding importance for this rule to be broken.

Not so in the artistic profession. According to the 'Show-Must-Go-On' axiom, *any* public performance is of overriding importance. The underlying idea is that the artist must not let down his colleagues, the promoter and, above all, the public.

This deserves closer examination. Unless there are special circumstances – for instance, the artist being one of those rare people who, due to some flaw in their mental make-up, are known to cancel appearances without good reason – experience shows that colleagues will accept the situation with good grace. After all, it might be their turn next. In some cases, a substitute can be found. If the artist is irreplaceable, there may well be insurance. At any rate, the occasional non-appearance is a fact of life normally appreciated by the artistic fraternity.

Naturally, promoters take a somewhat less relaxed view. The theory mooted occasionally by actors that the whole 'Show-Must-Go-On' syndrome is nothing but an invention by agents and theatre managements is intriguing yet hardly realistic. But these professions, too, recognise that the occasional cancellation is an inevitable 'law of nature';

indeed, I happen to know that most of them budget for an annual percentage of such cases. Of course, if they are let down too often by one particular artist, they will sooner or later write him off as unreliable.

Interestingly, a few promoters, when insuring against cancellation, sometimes stipulate that the artist in question must not be told of the policy's existence lest it should weaken his resolve to appear in the face of adverse circumstances. Whilst there is something in this, I believe it overrates the importance of insurance in the performer's mind. Conscious and sub-conscious motivations are usually stronger than merely practical or financial considerations.

And the public? Of course it is annoying to arrive at a theatre or concert hall only to find that the performance is off or that the star one had come to hear has been replaced by an unknown. But is it really more serious than, say, a train cancellation due to a wildcat strike or because a guard or driver has simply not turned up? This happens most days of the week – we have only to listen to early-morning radio or TV. It can cause inconvenience, hardship and even financial loss to more people and to a larger extent than the occasional cancellation of a public performance. But how do we react? We grumble, but we take it in our stride.

So the argument that the show *must* go on looks perhaps a little more threadbare than appeared at first glance.[26] In cases where one casts doubt on a long-standing well-established tradition it is often rewarding to try and trace its origin. This may not necessarily be as extreme as in the well-known story of the bench in a military barracks guarded, since time immemorial, by a sentry 24 hours a day; until someone had the sense to enquire after the reason. It turned out that, 100 years before, the bench had been freshly painted

---

[26] Incidentally, I am by no means alone in this opinion. Many years ago Noel Coward composed a chanson with the title quoted at the beginning of this section in which he made disrespectful fun of the matter (recorded on *Noel Coward in New York*, Columbia ML 5163)

and a sentry had been posted in order to stop anyone using it before the paint had dried (obviously the military commander of the day had no great confidence in the literacy of his men). It had simply been overlooked to cancel the order. A similar explanation seems unlikely in the case under discussion here. But could it possibly lie in the performer himself?

There are facts supporting this view. The missing train guard, for instance, is anonymous, the missing performer well-known; hence there is no public acknowledgement for the former, but keen appreciation for the latter who is working although he does not feel up to it. Then there is the artist's job satisfaction, the heady sensation of success without which some performers would probably not be able to function adequately – something entirely outside the train driver's experience. Third, there is the publicity, the glamour inherent in keeping his trust with the public – something again which is not granted to a train driver. And finally, there is the artist's egocentric make-up (an expression not used here in any derogatory sense), which may lead him to believe that his absence will be more deeply felt by his public than may be the case.

However valid these reasons, none of them seems to me to be strong enough to explain the lengths to which an artist may go in order to put in an appearance in the face of almost overwhelming odds and genuine hardship. I believe that there must be an additional far less obvious ingredient. But before I risk putting every artist friend's back up, let me reiterate that I am in no way wishing to disparage the tradition and motivation. All I am trying to do is to look at the phenomenon objectively. People often act in an admirable way for reasons which are not fully apparent to the outside world or even themselves.

It is my belief that in quite a number of cases – not, of course, in all – the subconscious motivation is a flight from reality. This enables the victim of a calamity to push it into the background, even if only for a short time, and instead to allow him to immerse himself in a somewhat unreal activity, which will demand his single-minded concentration and make him forget his immediate problems. It permits him to postpone action which, realistically, he ought to be taking right away. And last but not least, all this will earn him sincere praise for his dedication, having been able to convince the public and himself that what he is actually doing is more important than the realistic steps he ought to be taking.

Ridiculous? Fanciful? Far-fetched? Well, I at least don't know of any instance when an artist has ever been blamed for behaving in this manner. In one significant example, a famous artist, about to start a series of performances at an important festival, heard on the day preceding the premiere that his wife had been involved in a serious accident and that her life was in danger. Clearly, his place was at her side. But he chose to leave the show only after the first night – at the end of which he received an ovation for this dedication and heroism. But there can really be no doubt about the objectively relative importance of the two events.

And now imagine an ordinary business or professional man going to the office immediately following the death of a close relative. Would he not be condemned as unfeeling and heartless? And, for that matter, if he were to go on working while ill, would he not be accused of acting irresponsibly towards his colleagues, himself and his family? Yet there can surely be no doubt that the work of a solicitor or architect – looked at purely in terms of its necessity and urgency – is usually considerably more important than that of a performer. This has nothing to do with a comparison between the values of the artistic compared with any other profession, but solely with the question how realistically we react to a temporary interruption of one person's activities compared with another's.

Of course, one has to beware of over-simplification; there are a number of complicating factors. In the case of medical men, for instance, and especially surgeons, the overriding importance of an urgent life-saving operation is beyond question. A surgeon continuing his vital work in the face of an event which is for him personally catastrophic will earn high praise. But he might insist on cancellation for a different reason, fearing that the risk of his troubled state of mind might affect his concentration. Here, at least, realism wins the upper hand: the doctor's responsibility to his patient is recognised as more important than that of the artist to his public.

On the other hand, consider the case of a leading statesman faced with the problem of whether or not to cancel an important conference on account of a personal tragedy. Experience shows that normally he won't – although one might argue that it he were to commit a technical or political error he would be responsible to a far larger number of people than the surgeon to his solitary patient. On the other hand, the cancellation of the conference might affect the plans of many other persons, more important than the man in the street. And finally, a politician usually has the back-up of many experienced specialists, so that his own role may be less important than it often appears. In brief, there are many possible situations, so that most cases are not strictly comparable.

Altogether it seems extraordinarily difficult to bring all these contradictory features to a common denominator – which only shows that the problem is far more complicated than meets the eye. I should not be surprised if, as so often, the key is the public position of the person concerned. The mystique, the aura of unreality surrounding people in public life, seems to have been probed surprisingly little.

As a further point, the therapeutic effect of 'The Show Must Go On' should not be underrated – and not only for the artistic profession. I myself experienced this when, during the Second World War, I heard of my father's sudden death in Switzerland by reading, completely unprepared, in a London morning paper a brief paragraph headed 'CARL FLESCH DEAD. The report had been picked up from a Swiss broadcast the night before; a personal telegram reached me

only two days later. I telephoned a client to cancel an important appointment for that morning. This
caused such consternation and violent protests, with a complete disregard for my personal situation, that I eventually decided to keep the appointment; there was no possible communication with Switzerland, and absolutely nothing I could do. As I found out, the necessity of concentrating on an entirely different problem was probably the best method I could have devised to absorb the initial shock.

So why do I think that present trends point to a weakening of the 'Show-Must-Go-On' principle? To start with, there is an interesting antithesis, 'The show must *not* go on' as it were – the strike. Here everything possible is being done to prevent a 'show' (in the widest sense of the word) from taking place. Of course, the political and the artistic situations are completely different and it would be foolish to attempt a direct comparison between the two. And yet, some remarkable parallels are discernible; for instance, the firm conviction of the persons involved in the moral justification of their action (or conversely, inaction); their efforts to underpin it with realistic and idealistic reasoning; the not infrequently over-rated idea of the effect on the public.

To be sure, a striker usually makes a financial sacrifice, whereas an artist who keeps an engagement does the exact opposite – he saves his fee. But political considerations apart, I doubt that the financial question represents the main psychological motivation. For the artist, it is the job satisfaction; the effect on his public; and the flight from reality. As against that, a striker often finds his normal job anything but satisfying and welcomes a good reason for interrupting it. He receives no publicity for his work – except when he stops doing it; and he has the chance of temporarily neglecting the realities of everyday life, namely, the necessity of earning a living. It would be going too far to follow up the similarities and contradictions any further. But perhaps one day a sociologist will consider them sufficiently interesting to make them the subject of his thesis.[27]

The artistic profession itself, of course, is not free from events in which the principle is completely disregarded. Strikes by members of orchestra and chorus are today no longer as unusual as in former times, especially in the United States, where they are often an inevitable side effect of negotiations about the renewal of salary-scale agreements. This can pose severe problems, in particular for opera house managements, since internationally famous singers have to be engaged several years ahead of the performance date and usually demand a clause in their contract to the effect that they will receive their money even if the date of the engagement coincides with a strike.

And even individual artists do not always give the fullest consideration to the principle. As an example I can quote a somewhat startling entry in my father's diary:

The conductor Ansermet: 'No, I no longer believe in Casals'.

'Why?' Ansermet: 'I had a concert with him, in Montreux. He was to play the Haydn Cello concerto in the first, and the Don Quijotte (sic) solo in the second part of the concert. During the interval he says to me: 'Where is my fee? I always have to have it in the interval, otherwise I don't continue'.

Ansermet makes an urgent call for the cashier – he is not to be found. Casals: 'Well, then I won't play'. Another search. The audience is becoming impatient; catcalls and stamping of feet. Casals waits – at long last the cashier appears, hands Casals a bundle of notes. Casals, with the cello under one arm, counts the money – carefully, from time to time wetting his thumb with his tongue – the amount is right. 'Et maintenant nous pouvons continuer' -–mounts the platform and starts the solo with his enraptured Casals expression, '

---

[27]There may be other motivations, too. I am looking at them in number 19 dealing with class and the subconscious mind.

Depuis ce jour-là, je ne lui crois plus', Ansermet concludes.[28]

'Must the show go on?' the objective answer lies probably somewhere between the two extremes. But as a member of the public – and, to be frank, as a former insurance broker – my firm answer is: 'Yes, please, if at all possible!'

---

[28] Well, nobody is perfect. Casals' towering artistic importance is not diminished by an episode of this kind. The violinist Alma Moodie pertinently expressed it in a letter. 'You can't put all of it into words – I realised this again last week in a Casals concert in which he played like a God to a half empty hall. In the last resort it is not possible entirely to explain.'

11

A plea for artists' wives[29]

*"There is no higher praise
of a woman than not
talking about her."*

Chinese proverb

As the son of a concert violinist, I think I know something about the problems of artists' wives. Since I am writing only about matters of which I believe to have some knowledge, I shall be silent about female artists' husbands, except to say that their position is probably even more difficult than that of the wives, if only because the tabloids are more interested in them. We have only to think of the late Denis Thatcher. Though his wife was decidedly non-artistic, her other qualities compensated for that and he was by and large in the same position as a famous female artist's consort. The good humour, with which he coped, was admirable and, I think, exceptional.

Most spouses of busy and successful men, with the possible exception of those professionally engaged themselves; regard it as one of their prime tasks to spare their husbands the mundane day-to-day problems, so that they can concentrate on the weightier matters that concern them. In addition they will give them moral support where needed, and look after the social side, if this can advance their husband's career. Some, of course, will be working in their husband's business and give more hands-on assistance.

It is particularly in this latter respect, that the position of

---

[29] This is a revised reprint of a chapter from my book "And do you also play the violin?"

artists' wives is so different. The one thing they cannot do is to "help in the business". Of course, they can see to it that his wardrobe is always in top condition, well-pressed tails and clean shirts readily available; they can arrange for plane tickets, hotel reservations and visas; they may even, to a certain extent, take over the business side (though they should be careful not to meddle in matters that are the task of a professional agent; they usually lack the necessary detachment). But when it comes to the "business", the performance itself, there is no place for them, unless, of course, they happen to be part of an ensemble with their husband; but that is not the brand of artists' wives I am talking about. The genuine article just have to grin and bear it; the husband has to rely entirely on himself, they can't help him. This enforced inactivity leaves them powerless and may make them pretty frustrated. And that in turn can lead to an over-reaction: their unconditional loyalty and protectiveness may find an outlet in various ways that are regarded as greatly overdone, even annoying or ridiculous.

As long as the husband is at the top of his profession, this matters little, even if some wives allow his success to go to their heads. But there are few artists, however famous, who, from time to time, do not strike a bad patch. Even a Fritz Kreisler could occasionally be at the sharp end of a pretty unfavourable press review; sometimes damning him with faint praise: "Mr X was not up to his usual standard; we are used to perfection from him"). If this adversely affects their husband's self-confidence (artists do react in different ways) it is here, of course, that she must, whatever her own feelings, act as morale restorer. This is not always the case: the wife of Fritz Kreisler – I shall be referring to her several times, she seems to have been somewhat atypical – is said to have once entered the Green Room after one of her husband's performances, with the words "Today you played like a pig!" But if the story is true, it is certainly the exception.

And anyway, most interpreters cannot remain at their peak indefinitely. New names, new sensations pop up, threatening to overshadow the existing ones. These are the predicaments that tend to have the most marked effect on the wife. It does not necessarily make any difference whether the situation is real or imagined. The enthusiastic praise of another artist may already be perceived as an indirect attack. This can sometimes develop into an aversion against all his colleagues.

A prime example of severe "artists' wives syndrome" seems to have been the wife of the violinist Henri Marteau, who was very successful during the first decades of the last century, but whose reputation subsequently declined. My mother met her only once, at a tea party, which she happened to attend in the company of Mrs Kreisler. She reported amusingly about the occasion: "When she was introduced to us and heard our names, she simply turned her back on us, causing Harriet Kreisler to say in a loud voice: 'Who is this unpleasant person?' My mother, no slouch in these matters herself, could not forbear a malicious comment: "I have never forgotten the incident, because it was so funny. What poor Harriet did not realise, was that she herself was known as an "unpleasant person".

This, it has to be said, was not entirely without foundation. Kreisler had been, in his youth, according to my father who knew him well, an out-and-out Bohemian and in spite of his great talent might quite possibly have amounted to very little if he had not married Harriet who took him in hand and kept him under iron control. This undoubtedly helped him to the glittering career he so well deserved, but the price was that he remained completely under her thumb for the rest of his life, and everybody knew it.[30]

This brings us to the general question how far an artist's

---

[30] A famous story is that about Mrs. Kreisler being unwell and unable to attend one of her husband's appearances in a Furtwängler public dress rehearsal, which traditionally took place on Sunday mornings. "He was due on at 11.10. The Beethoven Concerto lasts 35 minutes. Applause 5 minutes. Green room 25 minutes. Taxi home 30 minutes. He should be back here at 12.45. It is now 1 o'clock. *So, where is he?*"

wife can affect her husband's career positively or negatively. I think, as I said before, that the Kreisler marriage was something of an exception. Contrary to what some people alleged, Marteau's career was not similarly affected, although his wife managed for him to break off relations with most of his colleagues at one time or another. But the effects of the wife's behaviour are limited, simply because the husband has the chance of escaping into a sphere where she cannot follow him, and where he gets the public approbation he deserves irrespective of how she conducts herself.

It has frequently been alleged that Yehudi Menuhin was another artist whose wife dominated his life. It is true that he was utterly devoted to her and showed it at every opportunity, but as far as my personal observation goes, I do not believe that this extended to influencing his career. He was an incurable idealist and what his wife did, was to try and keep his feet on the ground and protect him from the numerous people who tried to use him. This can, and in her case obviously did, create the wrong impression.

The conductor Bruno Walter, on the other hand, was known to have a very interfering wife. The story of a remark by the conductor Clemens Kraus deserves retelling: Kraus was involved in a discussion about his likely successor in Vienna. The name of Walter was mentioned. Thereupon Kraus: "Fidelio, act 2, scene 2" Somebody looked it up: the passage referred to is Leonore's outcry when throwing herself between her husband and Pissaro who is about to shoot him: "First kill his wife." However I am sure Kraus' mischievous remark did not influence the decisions by the selection committee one way or another.

Are artists' wives nervous before a husband's public appearance which they attend? This will partly depend on the latter's state of mind, but since – again according to my father – an artist *has* to be nervous to a certain extent, as long as it does not affect his technical skills during the performance, I think that, wives, too, are affected more often than not. I know my mother was. And I remember a symphony concert under Furtwängler at the Berlin Philharmonie, in which the violinist Adolf Busch was the soloist. I happened to slip into the management box just as he came on and encountered Mrs. Busch who was leaving. On seeing me, she said somewhat shamefacedly "Here goes Mrs. Busch." She was too nervous to attend a solo performance by him, whereas she apparently was all right when he played as leader of the famous Busch Quartet.

There is a lot of envy mixed up with the unfavourable way in which so many artists' wives are regarded. ("How did he come to choose *her*!") And let us not forget that performing artists as the favourite targets of adoring or simply scheming females are exposed to temptation more than the ordinary man, not least because they usually travel a great deal without their wives and therefore have a lot of opportunities. This is a very difficult situation for the spouses. They usually have to make greater efforts to hold their husbands than the wives of men in more mundane professions.

There can be, incidentally, an additional aggravation for the widow of a famous artist: that of being dropped by former acquaintances, which may have been fawning on her whilst the husband was alive. Sometimes she is left in no doubt that it was not she, but her late spouse, who had been the sole attraction and that now he has gone; she is of no further interest whatever. But even if people do not behave in this unforgivably cruel and tactless manner, it is inevitably very painful for her to realise how quickly the fame especially of a performing artist wanes and he is forgotten as the public transfer their allegiance to someone else who in the widow's opinion couldn't hold a candle to her late husband. She will do her utmost to keep the name alive. This can be very touching, but on occasion quite wearisome. The story of the widow of Franz Lehar, the composer of "The Merry Widow", is a case in point. In addition she had endless disputes with his publishers, which earned her in Vienna the title of "Die Lästige Witwe" – an untranslatable pun ("lustig" in German is "merry", "lästig" means "troublesome". The change of a single vowel completely alters the meaning).

Yes, being an artist's wife has its particular problems. It is for this reason that – warts and all – they deserve sympathy rather than the opposite reaction they so often engender. Leave them alone!

*

12

Enigmas

*"I would earnestly warn you against trying
to find an explanation for everything."*

Queen Victoria.

"I'll give you a definite maybe."

Sam Goldwyn.

An enigma is defined by the Oxford Dictionary as (inter alia)
"a mysterious or puzzling event". I would like for the purpose
of this section, to extend the definition and include events
which, at the time of their happening were neither puzzling
nor mysterious, but had very far-reaching consequences that
could not possibly be foreseen. Over the years, a sufficiently
large number of both kinds have happened to me or have
come to my knowledge from impeccable sources, to lead me
to the belief that to put it at its lowest, they may go somewhat
beyond the coincidental. Of course, we usually find our own
experiences more significant than those of others and this
may be so in my case too. But looking back, I find the
happenings sufficiently intriguing to relate a few of them.
Some, I admit, look insignificant in isolation, but I believe
that their accumulation makes them meaningful.

To me, non-puzzling events with unexpected far-
reaching consequences are as interesting as the other type. I
make no claim to originality. No doubt most of us must have
had this type of experience at various times. But unless the
connection is obvious, say the last-minute telephone call from
a long-lost relative that makes somebody miss a plane that
subsequently crashes, it may often go unrecognised. By
relating some that happened to me, I may trigger off

recollections of similar events in some of my readers' lives.

I will mention four, with one possible exception, all, as it happens, with favourable results. This does not, as some people might hope, point to a guardian angel, welcome though his existence would be, but seems to be a feature of these events, possibly because without them, some of us might no longer be here to tell the tale. In either case it shows up the utter unpredictability of life for all of us.

The first case, to which I have already alluded in a previous section, was the lame excuse I gave spontaneously and without thinking, when I was being taken to task by my teachers for being such an outstandingly bad pupil, especially since I was having to repeat the same form: "I know it all already and am simply bored". As a consequence I was put into the next higher class. So, this reply not only saved me one wasted school year, but also made it possible for me to advance my law training in Germany to a stage where its sudden termination by the arrival of the Nazis triggered off a substantial amount of compensation from Germany after the Second World War. One more year at school and I would probably have missed it. Doubtless the most lucrative innocent sentence I ever uttered. On the other hand, this is the one case that simultaneously had adverse consequences, namely the necessity for my parents to acquire German nationality essential for me to complete my studies. Due to my young age, I could not have been naturalised on my own. This caused them a great deal of trouble later, in fact put them in peril of their lives.

In August 1933 I emigrated from Germany to Holland. My mother was Dutch and I had quite a number of well-situated relatives and other good connections in that country, something that would doubtless have been helpful to me in my future career, not least because, as a refugee, I depended on any help I could get. I certainly did not dislike the Netherlands – the Dutch are, in fact, a very nice people, easy to get on with, and everybody was very kind to me; I even liked the language (most non-Dutchmen make fun of it, comparing it to a throat infection) – but I had a gut feeling that I did not want to stay there and formed a vague wish to go to England, where I had no connections of any kind. If I had been asked to say why I wanted to leave, I would have been at a loss for an intelligent answer: it certainly was not the proximity to Germany – nobody at that time dreamed of an invasion. Clearly, to give up a fairly certain future for an entirely uncertain one, without a really good reason, was the height of folly in my situation. But if I had taken the reasonable course, and stayed in Holland, I would, six years later, have been trapped by the German occupation and more likely than not, have suffered the terrible fate of so many other Jews – an extermination camp. Thus my action, at the time so entirely unreasonable, more likely than not saved my life.

A similar albeit I admit somewhat far-fetched instance. At the beginning of 1939, I had been 5 years in Great Britain and was therefore entitled to apply for naturalisation as a British citizen. On "day 5 years plus 1" my wife urged me to ask for the necessary application papers immediately. But I felt that this unseemly haste was a little undignified and deliberately postponed action for one month. The result was that at the outbreak of war in September 1939, the processing of my application had not been completed and, to our dismay, we had to spend the war as aliens. My application to volunteer for the army, made in the initial enthusiasm during the first days of the war, was refused on account of my former German nationality. But suppose I had become a naturalised Briton in time, I would no doubt have been accepted or have been drafted and my life might have taken an entirely different (and possibly much shorter) course. Obviously it is impossible to prove, but it is by no means unlikely that my idea not to rush matters, a mere foolish whim at the time, saved me from a "hero's death".

All these coincidences occurred comparatively early in my life; the only exception I can remember was a business matter. When – as described elsewhere – I took, at age 70, a job with a firm of Lloyd's brokers with a view to building up a German connection for them, a colleague asked me casually one afternoon whether I would care to sit in at a meeting with a security firm. There was no business in it, but it might add something to my knowledge. Having nothing better to do at that early stage, I agreed. Nothing in any way remarkable happened at the meeting, but more than a year later the official from the security firm whom I had met, did some business with a German banking association. One executive mentioned to him that they were looking for a bilingual connection with a London insurance broker. He happened to remember me, put me in touch and the business that resulted in consequence, was one of the most important I ever transacted and firmly established the position of myself as well as a colleague in my department. All that because I had had nothing better to do on that afternoon a year earlier.

Enough of that. Let me now turn to events fitting the more "conventional" definition of enigma.

To start with, again something comparatively minor, which, however, gave me much food for thought at the time, In his Memoirs, which I posthumously co-edited and published, my father described at some length his stay at Bucharest (1897-1902) as "Court Violin Virtuoso" to the very musical Queen Elisabeth, also well-known at the time (but now I think forgotten) as poetess under the pen name Carmen Sylva. Inter alia, he gave a brief description of the Queen's private concert studio where he quite often performed for her and her friends.

One day, when browsing through the stock of rare musical books and memorabilia belonging to my friend Herman Baron, a prominent dealer in these objects, I came across a photo of an ornately furnished room in which a distinguished-looking white-haired lady, whom I had never seen, was surrounded by a number of young girls in poses people adopted for photos 100 or so years ago. Without a moment's thought, I exclaimed; "This is the room in which my father made music for the Romanian Queen many times!"

And so it turned out. The lady was the Queen herself, with her ladies-in-waiting – they were listening not to a violinist, which might have given me a clue, but to a pianist, as I found out later, the composer George Enescu, equally skilled on the piano as on the violin. The striking thing for me is not the million to one chance of ever coming across such a picture at all, but the fact of instant and spontaneous recognition without a shadow of doubt or hesitation one would normally expect on such an occasion ("could it possibly be...?"), although there was no inscription on the picture giving a hint as to its identity or location. And I had had nothing but a word picture of the studio to go by, not sufficient by itself for me to recognise and identify the photo. I am convinced that there must have been more to it.

An experience that will give particular pleasure to adherents of astrology was told me by the son of a violinist to whom it had happened (and with whom I had in fact a slight personal acquaintance myself). He was of German origin, but had spent a large part of his life abroad. One day, in South America, he called on a concert agent whom he had not previously met. When they came face to face, it turned out that they were total look-alikes, down (or rather up) to a beard of exactly the same style. Not only that, but both had lost the sight in one eye as a consequence of a brain tumour operation. Both were professionally concerned with music – one as a performer, the other as an agent. And – you have, of course, guessed it – both had been born on the same day at the same hour. Make of it what you will.[31]

---

[31] But possibly the violinist had special gifts anyway. Many years later, I came across a letter to my father from the violinist Szymon Goldberg, in which he described that particular artist's violinistic technique. Apparently he had once played for my father who had referred him to Goldberg as a teacher, under his occasional supervision. The letter closed with the sentence: "With Paganini caprices" (technically among the most difficult in violin literature) "he shows a very good trait: he jumps blindly and usually hits the target." I believe there must be many a violinist envying him that somewhat supernatural gift.

Let us now turn to (alleged or real) communications from the Dead.

In the 1950s there practised a male medium in London, well known to the British public at the time through a series of BBC TV appearances, where he had, under strict scientific supervision, given a number of spectacular proofs of his capabilities. I had seen the programmes, had been very impressed and, after reading a long "profile" of him in the Sunday Times, that decided to consult him: I had been puzzled by certain aspects in the life of my brother-in-law who had died a short time before. I should perhaps mention from the outset that I left the meeting none the wiser in this respect, though this may have been due to the fact that, as I now recollect, I did not find an opportunity to ask the relevant questions, because quite a number of other interesting things had come up during the session.

I was told, for instance, that my brother-in-law had appeared, holding up some cigars and laughing – "it must be a family joke". I replied that I could not remember anything of this kind, and the matter was dropped. Only some time later did I remember an incident, which fitted perfectly and had put me into a very foolish light at the time – probably the reason why I had involuntarily suppressed it during the séance. Shortly after the war, I had visited my sister in New York. One day I asked a group of men in Times Square for directions. One man detached himself from the group: "I am going that way, I'll show you." During our walk he told me that he had been a GI during World War II and had been stationed in Luton. "Oh, did you by any chance meet a Mr. Bergman?" I asked. "Meet him! I became very friendly with the family and supplied them with silk stockings, cigarettes and sweets. How are they?" A friendly connection thus having been established on the basis of the "small world", we chatted amiably. Then he said; "I know that you British are not allowed to take abroad more than a minimum of currency (which was only too true). I am still connected with the army and able to get in our stores stuff very much more cheaply than the prices at which the general public can buy them. I would love to give you and your wife some cigarettes and perfume as a present." "Thank you very much, but that's out of the question." "Oh no, it would be a pleasure". This went on for some time, and eventually I said: "Well, it is very kind of you; tell me, how much would you spend?" "Ten dollars" (quite a large sum at the time, and certainly for me). "OK, here are ten dollars for you to use". I gave him my address and he promised delivery next day.

Coming home, I enthused to my family about the nice man whom I had met. "Are you telling me that you gave ten dollars to a stranger in Times Square?", my brother-in-law asked, roaring with laughter. "Yes," I replied somewhat nettled – after all, he had not asked me for the money, I had pressed it on him – and I bet you he will deliver the goods tomorrow." "I don't make bets with idiots," he answered. And, of course, the man never turned up, nor had Mr. Bergman in Luton ever heard of him. I was left somewhat in the position of the well-known tourist from the American West who, in London, buys a piece of the Nelson Column (or is it London Bridge) from a stranger. This became indeed a family joke at my expense. But except that it concerned cigarettes and not cigars, there can really be no serious doubt that this was the incident referred to.

Towards the end of the session the medium remarked suddenly: "I am seeing your father in the company of some bearded men and the name "Joseph" is coming up." "That's easy". I replied. "My mother's maiden name was Josephus-Jitta, and no doubt my father is spending some time with that family; all the men had beards at that period." It is, of course, well known that a medium will exploit this kind of information to the full. But not this one: "No, that's not it," he said. A relative who was with me at the session, remarked, half-jokingly: "Joseph Joachim?" (the doyen of German violin playing at the beginning of the 20th century, with whom my father had been acquainted; I have no doubt the medium had never heard of him; nor of my father). "Yes, that's it," he said. I thought this very funny at the time and for some years thereafter dined out on the story of my father playing quartet with Joseph Joachim in heaven, expressing the pious hope that the great man might occasionally permit him to play first violin.

Until I happened to meet one of Joachim's grandsons who was a retired school-teacher somewhere in England. I told him the story and expected the usual guffaws. Instead he said: "That's interesting. We have ourselves been "in touch" with my mother (Joachim's daughter and, like him a violinist). She has also told us that she is making music with her father. And in addition she has often mentioned the name of another participant: Carl. We couldn't think who he was." My father's first name was Carl. I would have loved to have independent confirmation from a third medium, but unfortunately the opportunity never arose. Still. It is a very intriguing coincidence indeed, if that's what it was.

The next story was told me by my friend Peter Diamand who for many years was the director of the Edinburgh Festival[32]. At a post- performance party of Mozart's "Figaro" at the Festival – Daniel Barenboim had been conducting, Peter Ustinov directing and there was a glittering cast – one of the members of the company claimed to be a medium experienced in table turning, and offered to give a demonstration. He made contact with a few family members of those present, resulting in the usual chitchat on these occasions, "How are you?" "I am very happy here." "Your mother is watching over you day and night and sends her fondest love", etc. "This is boring," exclaimed Ustinov. "I want Mozart." Mozart was duly summoned and indeed appeared. He was asked how he had liked the Figaro performance. "Very much, except for a certain orchestral passage (he gave details which I no longer remember), which should have been played by the whole cello section instead of only by its leader – unless it were to have been played by…"

---

[32] See also number 2.

and a chair moved rapidly in the direction of the cellist Jacqueline du Pré, Barenboim's wife who was of the party.

Thereafter, in order to test the authenticity of the phenomenon, Peter Diamand asked Mozart to name the first of his operas that had, several decades ago, been performed at the Holland Festival. "Don Giovanni," replied Mozart promptly. "Wrong. It was the Magic Flute," Peter replied; having been in charge of the programme at the time, he was in no doubt. "The Don". "The Flute." No agreement could be achieved and everybody left under the impression that the experiment had been at least a partial failure. Peter thought further about it and consulted some records, when he realised that it had been "Don Giovanni" after all!

My last case is an episode which I cannot regard as an enigma, but unashamedly call a miracle. In 1937 my father had two tickets for a Toscanini concert in London and, as my mother happened to be unwell, had offered one to me. I suggested that he take my fiancée instead – quite a sacrifice, but I was newly engaged and very much in love. On the day of the concert, I took them both to the Queen's Hall, at that time and until its destruction during World War II, London's foremost concert hall, in my little 2 door Morris Minor. On alighting my fiancée, who had been sitting at the front next to me, did not notice that my father was gripping the door post in order to draw himself up in order to get out of the car; she slammed the door with full force and *it closed, with my father's hand trapped.* I can still hear the noise of its closing. Of course, we opened it immediately and found that his hand was completely uninjured. This was confirmed – to make doubly sure –by a subsequent X-ray. I later tried the same experiment on my own hand and, of course. could not close the door at all if I were not to injure myself severely. By all the laws of nature and probability, my father's hand should have been completely crushed and his violinistic career (and presumably my engagement; neither my fiancée nor my family could possibly ever have felt comfortable with each other after this) have come to a tragic and irretrievable end.

To this day, I am utterly unable to explain what preserved him – but there it was. All our lives would have taken an entirely different turn, if the obvious had happened – but it didn't.

It bears saying once more: Much, though not all, of what I have written here, can be called commonplace. But can the same be said of the accumulation of it? I am half-convinced that there is "more in heaven and on earth...."

*

13

A human "time clock"? (1)[33]

"Die Zeit, die ist ein sonderbar Ding."

Rosenkavalier, Akt I.

I

Progress in genetic science has enabled us to recognise our genetic constitution to an ever-increasing extent, predict illnesses, identify physical weaknesses present and future and much else. In due course this will no doubt extend to many additional factors and characteristics. I believe that it is by no means impossible – indeed very likely, though to my knowledge so far not capable of proof – that our DNA somewhere indicates our constitutionally probable life span ("constitutionally probable", because no doubt medical science will enable us more and more to correct deficiencies that would previously have carried us off prematurely) and so to override the genetic prediction. And if it is true that such information is hidden within us, might it not be equally possible for our bodies and psyche, unbeknown to our conscious selves, to be programmed accordingly – that is to say to adjust the timing of our output to our originally predetermined life span?

I am not, of course, suggesting that those who achieve a great deal early in life, are bound to die prematurely. This idea would be as ludicrous as the opposite. But if there is any likelihood of our genes containing some kind of human clock regulating the length of our life, it is arguable that our life

---

[33] This is the almost literal reprint of an article published in Mensa Magazine in March 2004.

style and activities are equally programmed in accordance with the years allotted to us. This, at any rate, would go some way towards explaining why some people achieved so much in a very short life and conversely why long-lived people usually do not achieve *proportionally* rather more.. There might be in us an initial predetermined amount of capacity and productivity, which we are programmed to use to its fullest extent, exhausting it more quickly or more slowly according to the constitutionally predetermined duration of our life.

This is, of course, not in contradiction with our living to a mentally active old age. It is a home truth that, taking the right steps, mental capacity can be maintained in the same way as physical fitness. But just as in old age we are not able to accomplish physically anything like the same we did when we were young, there is no reason why it should be different where our mental capacity is concerned.

There are numerous examples of the output by, and the achievements of, people of genius bearing no relation to the length of their lives, neither in actual fact nor in our minds. We can mention Schiller and Goethe, Nietzsche and Kant, Mozart and Hayden, van Gogh and Rembrandt, Jane Austin and Longfellow, Schumann and Elgar, Chopin and Bach in the same breath without giving a great deal of thought to the fact that the difference in life span within each pair was in excess of twenty or thirty years. We do not feel – as our first reaction anyway – that the life's work of the shorter-lived in each pair is less "complete" than that of the other, just because he had fewer years in which to accomplish it. Thus it is obvious that in many cases the pure quantity of output bears no relation to the length of time within which it was produced. We usually feel that most geniuses have, as it were, "fulfilled" themselves even if they were with us for only a comparatively short time, except, of course, if they suffered an "un-programmed" accidental death, such as for instance the Belgian composer Chausson who, I am sure, would have produced a great deal more beautiful music but for a fatal bicycle accident.

Of course, there are not a few outstanding people living to a ripe old age, who achieved much both in early *and* in later life. But – disregarding the cliché of exceptions proving the rule – this might simply mean that their initial "stock" was abnormally large (after all, this is what made them outstanding), and that the clock regulating their output worked accordingly.

This is not always so. Clocks, both man-made and natural, can go wrong and be fast or slow. Consider on the one hand the "late developers" and on the other those who failed to "fulfill their initial promise". We have, in the latter respect, only to think of the many child prodigies in music, who sink without trace by the time they reach adulthood. Through some fault, they used up their capacity too quickly. Or of famous writers and composers – for instance Sibelius – who in later life produce work, if any, which bears no comparison to that which originally made them famous. Their capacity, too, had been used up prematurely. We even recognize this in our day-to-day language when we speak of people "drying up" or governments who have been in power for too long, having "run out of ideas". In politics, this is a harmless progression almost inevitably resulting in change of government at the next general election, unless their leaders happen to be dictators able to cling to power regardless of whether or not they have used up their potential; the catastrophic results are all too visible around us.

If my readers think all this highly improbable, perhaps I may ask them to consider this: if Shakespeare, Molière and others, during their comparatively short lives, could achieve their enormous output without the aid of a fountain pen, typewriter, let alone word processor, but probably still with a quill pen; if Christopher Columbus could discover America without the aid of an aeroplane – why is it that today's outstanding people, poets, composers, scientists, explorers, politicians, with all the modern technical means at their disposal, are not achieving immeasurably more than their forebears, in particular during the very much longer life time now granted them? Might this not be a further indication of a longer life span usually not having a direct effect on the quantity of our output?

So far, we have referred to outstanding personalities, because they are the examples on which we can best demonstrate the above theory, for what it is worth. But now let us turn to ourselves, the average people. Medical science has given us a considerably longer time to live, but does this mean that we normally achieve correspondingly more than our forebears? No, if we are honest, it doesn't. The ordinary lawyer, business man or whatever, looking back on his life's work, will rightly recognise it as not being superior in quantity or, for that matter, quality to that of his opposite number a few generations earlier, in spite of the modern advantages he has enjoyed (I except, of course, the medical and any other professions which profit directly from the progress of science).

I believe there is a simple reason: if we have more time, we take things more slowly. It is in the end nothing but good old Parkinson's Law: A piece of work expands with the length of time we have at our disposal to accomplish it, and vice versa. This we know to be true of individual tasks, so why should it not equally apply to a lifetime's work? And, if we think about it, it is even capable of a certain amount of indirect proof.

Since with all the technical means now at our command, we can complete our tasks more quickly than the generations before us, we have simply in a number of clever ways reduced the time we spend working or added tasks which we formerly found unnecessary. Who, a hundred or even fewer years ago, would have thought of the 5-day week, the 8-hour day (not to mention the 36-hour week), the frequent and prolonged holidays of today, the student's gap year? All this is not accidental, but has developed logically and some of it has in fact been decreed by those who govern us. As I write this I read of Britain being accused by Brussels of failing to uphold the EU Working Time Directive, which limits the working week to a maximum of, I believe, 48 hours. The European Commission has ruled that it is the responsibility of the employer to give employees the free time to which they are entitled and that the individual employee is not even free to choose to work longer! There are obviously a number of economic and sociological reasons for this (for one thing, there might otherwise not be sufficient work to go round leading to wholesale unemployment, but, consciously, Parkinson's Law is not one of them).

And added tasks? New supervisory bodies and quangos in the medical, legal, social, health and business fields are legion. Some (though not all) are necessary and desirable. But, again, the time clock may play its subconscious part in all this: we simply adapt, without realising it, the rate of our output as well as the amount of work created to modern developments. The desire for more free time in which to pursue our personal interests, is, whether we want to admit it or not, to some extent eyewash: many people don't know what to do with it and books have been written trying to teach them how to pass it.

Yes, we know much more than our forebears. But this is mainly based on the work of the people who came before us. Their inventions and discoveries were just as epoch-making as ours today. Whilst our knowledge has immeasurably increased, our capacity to make better use of it notwithstanding computers, mobiles, aeroplanes, motor cars, not to mention nuclear power, has not. Some of us may find this depressing, but should they? It is simply human nature, which in the end is stronger than any man-made plans or progress, so-called our genes.

.

II.

Can all the outstanding people who died at what was considered, even at that time, an early age, be said to have died "prematurely"? Yes, of course, if we regard the question purely from the point of view of their number of years on this earth. But their life's work is often anything but incomplete. As I believe to have shown, quantity and completeness of output often do not depend on lifespan. Yet the opposite is certainly the accepted view if we go by the so often-heard remark – "if only Mozart/Schubert/Mendelssohn had not died so young, how many more invaluable treasures would they not have contributed to our musical heritage!" So let us look at this a little more closely.

I have already indicated that by and large we do not regard Mozart's contribution to music as less complete than that of Beethoven's in spite of the fact that the latter lived about 20 years longer. This doesn't mean, of course, that if Mozart had lived to a ripe old age, he might not have continued to produce immortal music. But if what I said before has any substance, we cannot in fact be certain whether the further output by short-lived composers would all have been of the same value or whether their "human life clock" had been playing its part by having compressed the *rate* of output into the early years and used up the initial stock. I have to say that the mere suggestion of their standard ever falling, was, when I ventured to try it out on a number of musicologists not only regarded as utterly ridiculous, but as bordering on the blasphemous. Of course, by its very nature the matter cannot be proved one way or another. But the accepted opinion is obviously that they would not only have continued on the same level but in fact have developed even further and their additional output would, if this were possible, have been even more valuable, opening up ever new vistas.

I am not so sure, particularly about the latter: yes, they most definitely revolutionised the music of their period, but experience shows that after a time this becomes an everyday fact of life and other new ideas are required. It is exceedingly rare for revolutionaries to repeat this process however long they live. One revolution during a lifetime seems to be all even the most dedicated revolutionary is able to manage.

Yet, let us go along with the musicologists and assume that the additional output would indeed have been of equal or even greater value than that achieved so far. We now come to another and I suggest by no means less important practical question, which I believe cannot be all that easily pooh-poohed: would we really have been able to absorb, let alone appreciate a double or treble portion of Schubert songs, Mozart concertos and operas or for that matter Shakespeare plays? Would it even have been unquestionably desirable? The obvious answer to that is "why ever not!", but I make bold to suggest that we think again. There are a few matters that require clarification.

For one thing and not necessarily the most important one, works of genius are, in some way, "unique". Yet even the best things in life lose their uniqueness if there is an overabundance of them. But surely, you will reply, an "overabundance of works of genius" is a contradiction in terms. Maybe. But scarcity does play its undoubted part in the question of how much we value something. An apt example – if I may bring money into it – is the value of violins made by old masters. I remember that in the 1930s the market value of a well-known Strad, the Brancaccio (unfortunately destroyed in World War II during an allied air raid on Berlin), was £1,500. Whilst this is over 70 years ago, no amount of inflation can explain the difference between £1,500 and the value – many hundreds of thousands – it would have today. One of the very potent reasons is that there are, today, fewer and fewer good Strads in the world, hence the value of the individual article rises. But why should the opposite not be equally true? If someone were suddenly to discover a hitherto unknown stock of two dozen Strads, their value would go down (provided centuries of non-playing had not irretrievably spoiled the newly discovered treasure trove).

As I said, my opinion earned me nothing but contempt from those with knowledge far superior to mine. So let us assume (with them) that I am utterly wrong and turn to another question: would double the output have been all that desirable? Yes and no! No in the sense that the music loving public for whom these composers wrote, might not have been able to deal with it adequately. Needless to say, this does not question the fact that, on general grounds, it is to be regretted that these composers were not able to produce more, but merely that I am trying to look at the matter realistically. To put it at its simplest: if we had a double output of equal value by Mozart, what would have been the indisputable result? Would we have made, or listened to, more music than we do today? Of course not; all it would achieve is that every composition by Mozart would be performed, on average, only half the number of times compared to what it is today. As it is, we have already to make choices and cannot hope to absorb the whole output of any composer with a great many works to his credit. "Never mind that," you will say, "it is sufficient that it exists." Really? Music that is not being performed has at best a "half-life", if that.

Another thing: if my assumption of every single Mozart composition being performed only half as frequently is correct, seeing that there are twice as many as those he actually left us, would this be wholly desirable from other points of view? We would for instance have little or no time to listen to lesser composers who would be performed correspondingly more rarely if at all. Well, who needs them with all this divine music about in abundance. Are we certain, however, that we would like to be without or with considerably less of Mahler, Saint-Saens, Fauré, Grieg, Reger, Bruckner, Elgar? And who could say with certainty that concentration on a few geniuses, with other composers being neglected, would have been conducive to the development of music generally? Leaving this aside, if every one of Mozart's works were to be performed only half as frequently, it would deprive us of much *intimate* knowledge of certain masterpieces quite indispensable to us. *Cui bono?*

A minor but nevertheless valid point: what would be the effect on the record industry? The record companies, as far as they bother with classical music, have no need to add to their current woes by an over-abundance of material of equal value and attractiveness to a distinctly limited number of consumers. Thus, in order to make any record commercially viable they would have to neglect deliberately half the divine output or else they could never hope to make any money. So what is the point of heavenly music not performed anything as frequently as it deserves?

Thus, whilst regretting the early deaths of so many geniuses, let us be satisfied with what we have. It is more than sufficient for the lifetime of the ordinary music lover, who is after all, an important if not the most important, part of the equation.

*

14

Some blimpish thoughts on punishment.

> *"This is quite a three-pipe problem and I beg that you won't speak to me for fifty minutes."*

> Conan Doyle, Sherlock Holmes.

> *"I am all for bringing back the birch, but only for consenting adults in private."*

> Gore Vidal.

For hundreds of years, books and treatises have been written by philosophers, criminologists. sociologists and others about the ultimate purpose of punishment: retribution, deterrent, improvement (which of course, raises the question how this is best achieved), protection of society or a mixture? Can we say that all these deliberations have led to real progress? I dare not decide whether it is based on the "good old days syndrome" of an old man or actual fact, but frankly I cannot see much of it. On the contrary: all that seems to have happened is that crimes are becoming more numerous, fewer are being solved and sentences have become more lenient.[34] The last would in fact be a welcome development if at the same time positive steps were taken to make the criminals better people and so prevent them from re-offending, but, as a general rule, this does not seem to be the case either.

This has many reasons, from social enlightenment – justified as well as wrongly perceived, and passive rather than

---

[41] which seems somewhat to weaken a recent theory by scientists at the Zurich University that inflicting punishment creates pleasurable feelings in those who impose it.

active – via the simple overcrowding of prisons to an overworked police force. Nobody appears to be able to solve the many problems that continue to plague us, and this makes it all the more interesting to look at them anew and try to find different angles if possible.

There are criminals in all layers of society. Wrongdoing as such can be either "classless", as for instance sexual offences, blackmail, the activities of conmen, drug dealing, fraud, etc., though there may be differences in sophistication and size; or – and I think in the majority – "class-related" in the sense that it is committed by members of certain classes more frequently than by others. And since below the line the majority of criminals belong to the poorer classes, it follows that crime and class must often be interconnected. You will normally not find a burglar or mugger among well-to-do people simply because they do not need to rob or steal – their education and upbringing has enabled them to make as much money by (not necessarily more legitimate) different means. And the reverse is equally true, vide tax cheats, dishonest company directors and the like – crimes in which the poorer members of society have, for obvious reasons, no interest. Again, crimes of violence are likely to be more frequent among the latter, presumably because they were not taught in their youth, by example or otherwise, to use alternative means of expression.

What can we deduce from this? If the types of criminals and crimes are different, it follows that the kind of punishment as well as its purpose should be different, too. No prison sentence, however severe, would make the Maxwells, Archers and Aitkens of this world "better" or for that matter "worse" people. They were originally successful in what they did in a legitimate way and made their conscious and reasoned choice whether or not to, as it were, "add" criminality, something for which there was no real economic need. They can neither be improved by a custodial sentence, nor is there in most cases any particular necessity to protect the public from them in this way. Incidentally, tagging people like this after release, as I believe is done with increasing frequency, is a ludicrous exercise, which cannot possibly do any good to anybody, but is a waste of time and effort that would be better directed towards more effective, means of combating crime.

Deprivation of liberty is, of course, a deterrent, not only for the obvious reasons, but partly also because of the stigma attached to it. But this latter point should not be over-rated; the real criminals do not regard it as such, and it is equally open to doubt whether it even plays as decisive a part as it is supposed to do in a number of other cases either. Many of the people involved more or less regain, after they have served their time, their former place in society, in particular if they are prominent, such as Saunders, Archer et al.

It would be equally futile to impose any other *mild* punishment on these classes, such as a comparatively small fine, or community service with reform in mind. If, in the latter case, this is not the purpose, it must be humiliation; the modern equivalent of stocks in former times. What else does one expect from it? If, as I maintain, prison does not always serve as a deterrent, well-to-do people can be hurt mainly by a really severe fine and wide powers of confiscating assets (monetary or other) that they have been able, through their criminal activities, to stash away or transfer to spouses, other relatives, friends or partners, even when these people were not necessarily in the know. This might be coupled with an official ban from, following for a time the occupation that gave them the opportunity for the offence they committed (preventing them for some years from being company directors is not good enough). Apart from being a real deterrent, a really large fine would save the state much expense in money and manpower; if I am not mistaken, the cost of keeping a prisoner exceeds that of a stay at an AAA-rated hotel. If, a prison sentence is imposed, well-to-do criminals should be made to pay for its cost at a realistic rate.

However, it seems to me that in practice a different scale of punishment is often applied: the more, for want of a better word, "civilised" the crime, the less severely the retribution is likely to be. It therefore fails in its purpose – deterrent. That is not very likely to change until we make it a principle that crimes by people not financially deprived or occupying a high social position, ipso facto deserve the more severe punishment for that very reason. If this sounds draconic, so be it, if it helps to reduce the wealthy-class-related crimes.

In fact, this is not by any means such a new idea: we often punish, for instance, bent policemen or medical men who have abused their professional status, more severely than others precisely because, as the presiding judge will not fail to emphasise, they violated a trust. By the same token, people who occupy high social positions and/or can "afford" not to be criminals, have, or should have, an equal social responsibility and ought to be treated accordingly. Like policemen and doctors, they deserve not lesser, but more severe retribution. This opinion may not be very popular with the "establishment". Well, not to worry, there is no sign that any such reform is likely to take place in the foreseeable future. But it is worth thinking about.

As already mentioned, crimes committed by the middle and upper classes are in the minority. How to treat the bulk of criminals, remains the far bigger and more intractable problem. In theory the solution ought to be comparatively simple: those, for whom there is any hope of reform, should be treated differently from those for whom there is no such expectation. But apart from this method possibly offending against Human Rights legislation (I am not sure about that, but nowadays almost everything does) it is in practice usually not possible, to make the required distinction with any certainty. In consequence, some criminals who cannot be reformed would be treated too leniently, whereas others who could be, would not only be denied the opportunity, but on the contrary be sent to the "schools for crime", the prisons. The short-term answer might be for judges, in more cases than at present, not to pass sentence immediately but to await a social services' report. Unfortunately, here, too, it must be open to considerable doubt whether the knowledge and skill of today's average social worker would be remotely up to the task. And anyway, for this to work, an extended reform programme for criminals would have to be created simultaneously. My suggested differentiation in sentencing could obviously not work without it. Perhaps this is where we ought to start with our reform programmes?

It is, incidentally, an established fact that crime in countries under dictatorship or in very strictly religious communities is less frequent than in others, either because there is a greater sense of moral responsibility or simply because there is a more effective deterrent: punishments are sometimes quite unpredictable or inhuman and the onus of proof is often less severe. Is, then, a dictatorship or at least a police state the answer? Of course not, for obviously their disadvantages outweigh any possibly advantageous by-product, whether it is more punctual trains or fewer criminals. Maybe we shall have to leave the solution to an improvement in the living standards of the bulk of the population, so as to make crime a less attractive or necessary option all round. But this, too, is, of course utopian.

So, is there no way out? Well, it can hardly be denied that there was, in former times, a stricter moral code, mainly based on the teachings of the various religions. As we all know, this factor has largely disappeared. It should be up to the authorities to replace it by a "secular moral code", but this idea is in total conflict with the often so misunderstood more liberal attitudes of today. Only when a government has the courage and authority to withstand the inevitable ridicule such teachings would initially engender in "enlightened" circles, and to use the full publicity power of the press and TV for promotional purpose, can there be any hope of progress: admittedly, an expectation as utopian as that of material improvement all round, but hands up those who have a better idea.

Why are street crimes still so much in the ascendancy? One of the obvious reasons is the present under-manning of our police forces and as a consequence the disappearance of the bobby from the streets. Constant efforts are being made to remedy this, but until politically correct red tape is reduced and manpower is freed, real progress is unlikely. Most of these types of crimes cannot be solved and it is therefore in the interest of the authorities not to make too much of a fuss about them. Thus, what is being emphasised nowadays is the reduction in crimes in some other areas or in total, the increase in violent crimes being played down.

But scarcity of policemen on the beat is only part of the problem. There is also the allegation of "institutional racism" that is bound to affect the work of the force. It goes without saying that racism, whether in the police or elsewhere, exists and must be condemned in all its forms. But let us be certain of what we mean by it. Surely there is a vast difference between (a) disliking certain races and (b) acting unfairly against its members for that reason alone. There is no reason why (b) has to be a consequence of (a) something that, to go by newspaper reports, seems often to be disregarded by the authorities, anxious to be politically correct. We live in a free county and cannot be punished for what we think, however mistakenly, as long as we do not act in accordance with our mistaken beliefs. There seems to be an opinion abroad that policemen cannot be trusted to make this distinction.

This attitude is bound to hamper severely both the work and the function of the police. If it is true that there is a connection between crime and poverty – and of course there is – it follows that, percentage-wise, more coloured people are likely to commit crimes than white ones, simply because, at present, there is a larger proportion of poor in the black than in the white races. For a policeman to hesitate to stop and search a coloured person because he fears trouble as a racist is simply counterproductive.

Let us now turn to the rights and wrongs of the death penalty. This has always been one of the most controversial subjects, and I believe still is, notwithstanding the fact that a parliamentary majority and an enlightened public opinion are against it. It has been abolished in this and many other countries as unsafe, inhuman and violating the rights and dignity of man. It is also being alleged in some circles that its abolition tends actually to reduce the number of capital crimes, because some criminals have a subconscious death wish and are therefore attracted to crimes that carry the death penalty. Possibly so, but there must be vastly more people for whom it is a greater deterrent than a "life" sentence. It is further said that the carrying out of a death sentence is dehumanising for the executioner as well as for all of us. Let us look at all this and be as politically incorrect as we like.

For me, the strongest argument against the death penalty has always been the possibility of a miscarriage of justice that cannot be corrected. Cases where this did occur in the past are well-documented. On the other hand, there are capital crimes, for which, if proven beyond any (i.e., more even than reasonable) doubt, this objection simply does not wash. For instance I feel it is the only suitable punishment for anyone convicted for the murder of a child, of more than one person, let alone of 3500 as on 9/11 or, for that matter, any terrorist act affecting innocent people. You do not have to subscribe to the "eye for an eye, tooth for a tooth" doctrine to acknowledge that there are criminals beyond the possibility of redemption and/or for whom nothing but death is the proper punishment. Nor can I see, with all the unrelieved poverty in this world, why the State should fork out immense sums of money to keep for decades an entirely worthless life that can never again be of the slightest use to society or itself. If, with the same expenditure, half a dozen lives can be saved by cutting NHS waiting lists, surely this would be preferable?[35]

Hence, I am not opposed to the death penalty in certain circumstances, but I would introduce a number of reforms and safeguards that deal with the present objections: (1) death sentence not to be mandatory for *any* crime; (2) scrutiny by an independent panel of forensic and legal experts as well as respectable laymen before any death sentence is carried out, it being automatically remitted if the *slightest* doubt remains. And (3), I would make the execution itself more humane. The purpose of the death penalty should be to remove an entirely worthless member of society for good, but not to do this in a quite unnecessarily barbaric and cruel manner, such as electrocuting, hanging, gassing, or beheading.[36] Today, you can,

---

[35] I am reminded of the teachings of some self-improvement manuals which give the advice to "concentrate on your strengths" rather than on your weaknesses. The latter, they maintain, is wasteful because the result, even if you achieve improvement, will even at best never take you above average. Why spend so much effort on something, for which you cannot expect a really good return, instead on something, that has a chance of much greater success? Why should the principle of concentrating on one's strengths not apply to the State as well as individuals?

It goes without saying that I am not advocating to give up on, let alone destroying, other "useless lives", i.e., those of the severely handicapped, whether still worth anything to society or not. They got into this situation though no fault of their own and it is the State's full responsibility to look after them regardless of cost. What we are dealing with here, are persons who, (a) are shown to be worthless and irredeemable and (b) have got into this situation through their own severely criminal action, deliberately doing incalculable damage to others.

[36] I include in that any ceremonial such as the reading out of a sentence to the accused in full view of the gallows, which can only prolong the agony. I remember visiting after World War II the well-known Plötzensee near Berlin, where the Nazis had carried out a large number of death sentences on enemies of the State. The atmosphere of this place was, after 25 years, still physically oppressive. The accumulation of extreme fear of death of the many victims still hung over it.

prior to an operation, send anybody painlessly to sleep in the space of three seconds. Why not do the same before an execution and then apply a further, lethal injection on the unconscious person? Any other method smacks of the Middle Ages.

We are all of us under sentence of death from the day we are born. But we don't know when the sentence will be carried out and therefore are programmed not to live in constant fear of it. A death sentence removes this uncertainty and the fear engendered thereby is part of the punishment. There is no need to add to it.

At the same time I cannot see any objection in principle to executing someone who was sane when committing his crime but has meanwhile become insane (and good for him, he may in fact no longer realise that he has to die on a certain date). Does insanity make him a better person or more deserving of care? Surely, it is the state of mind at the time of the crime that matters. I am not sure whether to believe the Alice in Wonderland story of the American authorities in one case doing their best to bring an insane man back to sanity with the sole purpose of executing him after he had regained it. This is simply beyond any reason and a good example of where such misinterpretation of reality can lead.

What about young children who have committed wilful murder? They can obviously not be executed, but at the same time they have, in my firm opinion, to be permanently removed from society. They have shown that they lack certain normal and socially indispensable controls and inhibitions and, in the present state of medical science – which, in this sphere, will surely continue for a long time to come – one can never be certain that they can really ever be cured or reformed. I agree that in many cases they cannot be held criminally responsible. But to free them, ever, for this reason, is not a risk the State should be allowed to take in the interests of society in general whose rights, in this instance, have precedence.

I am thinking of the two most striking cases in recent

years, the Bulger and the Huntley murders. In the first, two little boys aged about eight were detained for an indefinite period for a particularly cruel killing of another child. But I gather that they were subsequently set free. The authorities went to immense lengths and expense to give them new identities so that they could not be recognised, but on the contrary would be enabled to lead normal lives. No doubt it was considered that they were no longer a danger to society – but, as I have pointed out, who can really be certain? What a frightful idea for anybody to become friendly, socially or otherwise, with a brutal child murderer; or, even worse, for those boys to marry unsuspecting girls and produce children of their own who might well be at risk. To bring this situation about, is plain crazy.

Now compare this with the second case, that of the fully adult James Huntley who murdered two little girls. He had been employed as a school caretaker in spite of his past record of under age sex and more serious sexual offences (though in the latter case there had not been sufficient proof to lead to his conviction in a court of law). Prior to engaging him, his prospective employers had very properly instituted the necessary enquiries and had been told by the police authorities that nothing untoward was known against him. If the relevant information had been given, this would have prevented him from obtaining, probably any, and certainly the particular job that brought him into continuous contact with children. An enquiry was held afterwards how and why such a slip-up occurred and to make sure that such a thing cannot happen again. Obviously the correct attitude. But can anybody tell me how this tallies with the Bulger case, in which every effort is being made to achieve precisely the opposite result, i.e., to make sure that the boys' past will not ever come do the knowledge of anybody? How can you condemn this in one case and do precisely the same in another? These attitudes are diametrically opposed and both cannot possibly be right. Just imagine if one of the Bulger boys had successfully applied for Huntley's job!

The Bulger boys and others like them must not be set free, because there is always the risk of their remaining a danger to society. It is as simple as that. I would regard what they did as a tragedy not only for the victims and all families concerned, but for them as well. If they had been adults, they would have suffered a very severe penalty. They didn't get punished – rightly, because of their youth – but they cannot, under any circumstances, ever be trusted and allowed back into society; the risk is too great. True, if their past becomes known whilst they are free, their lives will be ruined. If it is successfully concealed, then the public is misled. Who on earth can be in any doubt what is worse? As I said, a tragic situation for them. There is no way out of this dilemma: without making *someone* suffer; it is entirely logical that this must be the perpetrators of the deed. If the Bulger boys, instead of murdering a playmate, had been run over by a bus and become paraplegics for life, unable to move, work or to look after themselves, it would have been equally regarded as a terrible tragedy, but these things, unfortunately, do happen and we have to deal with them in the light of the circumstances pertaining. I would place their misdeed in exactly the same category as the bus accident: a tragedy making them unfit for a useful place in society and deal with it accordingly. There is, of course, every reason to treat the boys humanely, but that has nothing to do with the risk of setting them free. There might, again, be some "Human Rights" implications – but nobody can deny that any other way does, on the balance of possibilities, more harm than their life-long detention.

There is yet another contradiction in this sphere – the case of the serial killer Dr. Harold Shipman who in the absence of the death penalty, which he thoroughly deserved, was condemned to life imprisonment but managed to take his own life shortly after commencing his sentence, apparently for the (I think laudable) purpose of giving his innocent wife the benefit of his life assurance. Some people – some of them probably the same who are in favour of the death penalty –

complained that he had "cheated" and had "escaped" his punishment. But whilst part of the purpose of life imprisonment was retribution, its main and more important aim was the protection of the public. From this angle, it does not make the slightest difference whether and for how long he was going to live in captivity. By taking his own life, Shipman carried out the death sentence on himself, which many people felt he deserved but which the judge could not legally impose on him.

This has led to an interesting suggestion by a respected commentator: he proposed that in appropriate cases a criminal should be given the choice of taking his own life if he so wished. I think that – again subject to proper safeguards – this is not all that bad an idea. But in accordance with present-day practice, everything is being done to prevent such a solution. There is a "suicide watch" on such people to prevent them from doing away with themselves. In the Shipman case it was obviously not carried out as meticulously as, in the opinion of the authorities, it should have been. A time-consuming and no doubt very costly investigation is being held in order to prevent such a terrible thing happening again. It is said that the criminal, however worthless, has to be "protected against himself", and has to be given "proper care". Of course he has, but why go over the top?

The attitude towards crime, criminals and punishment is full of contradictions and unsolved questions. It is to be doubted that clear solutions will be found in the foreseeable future if ever, but this is an added reason for keeping the problem constantly in mind.

*

15

Emergencies and emergencies.

"Not seeing the trees for the wood."

If we read of a disaster such as a trapped submarine crew, mine workers buried in a collapsed seam, the unexplained disappearance of a little child, a climber stranded with a broken leg on a snowy mountain ledge; or even of comparatively trivial happenings,–such as a little dog down a well, a whale stranded somewhere on the coast; not to mention two pre-teenagers absconding (though I think, this can hardly be classed as an emergency); our reaction is automatic and inevitable: we expect immediate action, and this is unhesitatingly taken by the powers that be or the relevant rescue organisations. The question of cost, chances of success and the amount of effort needed are completely disregarded by all concerned. Lifting gear is assembled from all over the country, rescue or search parties sent out, salvage ships and planes are called up, large police forces are committed, and so on, the list is endless.

This is, of course, as it should be, but let us not delude ourselves: in most cases the scope of the action taken is quite out of proportion to the *objective* importance of the event. Never mind! Common humanity and public sentiment demand it and the appropriate organisations rise to the occasion "without hesitation and contradiction." If they didn't, there would be hell to pay. I can recall offhand only one case where a Government refused to take *every* possible action in a situation of this kind: that of the Russians when one of their submarines got stuck at the bottom of the sea. They refused the foreign help offered as pointless. As it turned out their judgement had been entirely realistic, but the world reaction was devastating. I should not be surprised if in a democratic country such an attitude, whatever its rights or wrongs, might almost be sufficient by itself for the Government to lose the next general election without really trying.

I would, I repeat, not dream of criticising this urgent wish to do everything humanly possible. But if we think about emergencies generally a little more deeply, we come across an interesting phenomenon: public reaction and measures taken, speed, size and cost are frequently not only not commensurate with the size and objective importance of the event (disregarding of course, the subjective one for the individuals concerned and their families) but can even be said to be in inverse proportion thereto. Events such as the famine in some African countries threatening the lives of millions; the number of aids cases in some others (or for that matter the same) undermining the future of whole generations; the unspeakable atrocities committed by many dictatorships and so on – they are objectively and undeniably of far greater moment than even a mining or U-boat tragedy. Nor can we claim not to be fully aware of them; they are regularly shown to us on our TV screens and are extensively dealt with by the local or special correspondents of our media.

Of course, we are greatly touched by them. Yet, with few exceptions, it cannot be said that they engender the same intense emotional involvement and passion as the type of events mentioned in the beginning. We contribute to the various charitable appeals by organisations trying to alleviate the suffering; and, equally, most of us applaud our Government for making large amounts of money, goods and services available. These are intended to help millions of people, but compared with the amounts spent on the attempts to save just a handful of individuals in danger of their lives, they are, of necessity, often quite negligible. By this I mean that the millions provided in the case of a famine may amount to, say, £5, £10, with luck even £15 per victim, whereas the cost of trying to save two individuals stranded on a mountain ledge may easily run into £25,000 each, if not more.

Whichever way we look at it, there can be no doubt that this represents an enormous discrepancy. Yet there appears to be no public awareness of this. Whether large or small, *both* types of event are without doubt emergencies of the first order, but the larger the catastrophe, the less it is regarded as something requiring the same urgency in dealing with it. The exceptions are natural catastrophes such as hurricanes, earthquakes and bush fires; but these, of course, require immediate action often for the simple reason that otherwise they might get entirely out of hand and cause far greater loss of life and property. One of the more recent examples is, of course, the unique Indian Ocean Flood catastrophe, with its immediate and magnificent response by both public and governments. Yet I do believe that even here, the gut feeling and emotional involvement of the general public was not as strong as, for instance, in the case of a hostage taking, be it of one or two individuals or a whole school or theatre audience. Why should that be so?

There are, several, realistic reasons for this different attitude. One of them is purely logistic: the sheer size, which, we realise, makes complete and/or prompt remedial action for instance in Africa far less viable than in the case of a smaller event. Clearly, you cannot lay your hands on hundreds of millions as easily as on a comparatively smaller amount, nor hope to help an enormous number of people at the same speed as two or three or twenty. But this factor ought not necessarily to influence public sentiment and the gut feeling calling for immediate action in large catastrophes as well.

And yes, of course, distance has a lot to do with it, too. Many of the really enormous catastrophes seem to occur[37] in, for us, remote parts of the world whereas those that grip us so forcefully usually happen very much nearer home. Yet, even

---

[37] Since writing this, we have, of course, experienced Hurricane Katrina. The initial adverse public reaction to the measures apparently neglected – I can make no judgement whether justified or not – was, I believe, partly due to the stress laid by the media on individual cases and also to the fact that the catastrophe occurred on America's doorstep.

events happening on our own doorstep do not engender the same demand for urgent action. The waiting lists of the NHS, which affect hundreds of thousands, will show what I mean. This is not a political pamphlet and I am certainly not sufficiently qualified to treat the reader to yet another critique or opinion on how the NHS should be reformed. I just like to use it as an illustration of the phenomenon of the feeling of urgency in the public mind being in inverse proportion to the size of the catastrophic event.

If we were to come across a news item headlined "Another 50,000 sufferers from dangerous heart complaints have to wait nine months for NHS treatment" we would no doubt feel highly indignant, but the thought that this probably means early and unnecessary death for a few thousand people, would not be our first reaction. It would, after all, probably be less than 5%. We would very likely shake our heads and turn the page possibly even thinking something like "what else is new". Now replace the words "50,000 sufferers" with "a pensioner and war hero", leaving the rest of the item unchanged. I am prepared to bet that we would not only take far more notice of the story, but expect immediate action to remedy a catastrophe whose size is .002 % of the first-named one. Should it not be the other way round? 50,000 emergencies, for this is what they are, compared to one! Haven't we got our priorities wrong?

Yes and no. The reason why we react so differently is the fact that we are told that the big problem is being worked on and that we realise that an immediate solution is impossible. So there is no point in getting too hot under the collar about it. We may think, according to our political orientation, that the Government is not doing sufficient or not the right things, but we arc not thinking of an immediate revolution, only of the next general election, two years away. We are probably not satisfied, but we accept, even if grudgingly, the explanation that currently there are not the technical means and/or personnel available to help so many waiting list victims, but that, all being well, it is hoped that

179

within 12 months, the waiting lists – the emergencies – will have reduced by 10%. If only one or a small group of persons were concerned, that would simply not be good enough. Fancy the authorities in the case of the stranded climber stating that the matter was being urgently and carefully considered from every angle and that they were working on a decision about the best new type of helicopter capable of lifting injured climbers off mountain ledges much better and more safely than the present ones can; the men would just have to hang on until the new method was up and running. I realise that this comparison is quite ludicrous, yet that is what we are regularly being told in respect of the hundreds of thousands emergencies – which, incidentally, no doubt include hundreds of war heroes. And what is more, we accept it as normal and inevitable. "TINA" – there is no alternative. And I have to admit that, beyond stating the stark facts, there is very little I can think of myself that might provide a real solution.

Which still leaves the question of an explanation of the comparative difference in intensity of the public reaction. I think that one of the reasons is that 50,000 people are "depersonalised"; whereas one or a small group of persons are not; hence we react differently. The way our mind is constructed, we simply cannot grasp facts properly unless they are expressed in such a way that we can relate to them in personal terms – until they are cut down to size. We keep large and small events in different, almost watertight compartments, as it were. If we are told on TV of a large-scale military action in which there were only 5 casualties, we are apt to think, "Only five, well, that's not too bad". If we heard of only two of them being in mortal danger of a different kind, our reaction would be the opposite. I am not in any way criticising this attitude. It is human nature, the way in which we protect ourselves – have to protect ourselves – against the bad news (good news is no news) with which we are being unceasingly bombarded on TV and in the press. I don't know how it was 200 years ago, but I have a suspicion that today's instant communication now at our disposal has blunted our conception in pure self-defence.

And not only that. There are, as I said, matters that are simply beyond our comprehension. Who of us can really visualise the universe, the cosmos? I had – on a rather lower plane, of course – a significant experience of this. In the course of my insurance career I became, for my sins, an underwriting member of Lloyd's, a "name" as they are called. Names accept unlimited liability for the losses Lloyd's incurs, "down to your last cufflink" as the saying goes. As may be recalled, Lloyd's made enormous losses for almost two decades, which cost many people all they possessed. Thereafter it was decided to introduce limited liability. When I was told the limited figure for which I would be liable, I realised for the first time the enormity of the potential loss and reduced my participation. As long as the liability had been unlimited, it was beyond my imagination and therefore did not properly register, only when it appeared in the shape of a concrete figure obviously much lower than "unlimited" did I realise its real nature. I believe there is a similar mechanism in our minds separating large from comparatively small catastrophes.

So, to repeat the question, is there really nothing we can do in the case of large emergencies? Are we certain that our rulers could not do better if pressed harder? Perhaps there is a partial answer: to try and "personalise" these events by dividing them into many smaller ones, so that they become better manageable both in our minds and in reality. It would certainly be nothing like a "cure-all". But even a little is better than nothing at all. To return to the NHS waiting lists; there are obviously cases more urgent than others – life threatening in real terms. If there were a separate body assessing them on application and if deciding that the emergency warranted it, to allot them to a special additional emergency unit, this would not mean jumping the queue – nobody would be disadvantaged – yet cases of real hardship would be helped more quickly. Another possibility would be to divide waiting lists into districts, hospitals even; they would immediately appear to be more manageable. By the same token large famine areas might be divided into smaller districts, and so on.

At the moment we have become set in our ideas that large catastrophes can only be solved slowly. I believe something could be done to speed this up. Only nibbling at the edges of the problem? So what! Every life saved is not a statistic, but a real person.

*

16

Relations with Germany

How long can you keep it up? [38]

> *"Now Hatred is by far the longest pleasure,*
> *Men love in haste, but they detest at leisure."*

Byron

To make it clear from the outset, this section is not about sexual performance, but about something that may be regarded as less pleasurable, but is certainly more fundamental: our relationship to present-day Germany and German citizens. It is a theme not only of importance to the special group of former refugees from Nazi persecution, but I believe to everybody.

In the mid1970s a German concert impresario, with whom I was on friendly terms, asked me whether I would mind, as a favour to him, asking the famous American violinist Isaac Stern (with whom I had the privilege of a slight acquaintance) to undertake a concert tour through Germany; Stern had decided never to appear there again. Whilst I did not consider trying to persuade him to change his mind a particularly worthy cause, the matter did intrigue me and I decided to write to him. The question whether and if so to what extent, to recommence relations with Germans, was, of course, a very acute one among us refugees, and opinions differed wildly. Stern, however, had been neither a German nor a refugee, and I was interested in the opinion of such a

---

[38] This is an amended reprint of a chapter in my (specialised) book "Where do you come from?". I felt that it might be of interest to a wider circle of readers.

prominent fellow Jew who had not gone through the same traumas as we had,

Accordingly, I pointed out to him that no German born after 1930 could have made a reasoned decision to become a party member (even if he had been in the Hitler Youth); a considerable proportion of the older generation were, through natural causes or as war casualties, no longer alive; in addition, there had been, after all, quite a few non-Nazis in Germany. Hence, I calculated that at most 20% of the present German population could still be called former Nazis and, since there were doubtless quite a few who genuinely regretted the past, it was fair to assume that the proportion of anti-Semites in Germany did not exceed 20% either. "Name me," I concluded, "a single country not necessarily excluding Israel where anti-Semites number fewer than 20% of the population. If you were to play only in countries with a lower percentage, I am afraid you would have had to give up playing in public long ago, even in USA and what a loss that would have been to music!" Stern, not averse to flattery, was good enough to reply that my argumentation was quite logical, but not sufficiently strong to make him change his mind. Germany was, for obvious reasons, a special case to which reasoned thought could not apply, especially for Jews. I heard afterwards that his wife had lost several relatives in the Holocaust, thus there had been an additional personal motive for his attitude. There was nothing further I could or wanted to say.

However, the story had an interesting and somewhat unexpected sequel. Many years later, Stern actually did agree to work in Germany in the form of conducting master classes at a music academy, in public, so that listeners were admitted. When it was pointed out to him that there could not really be any difference between public performing and public teaching, in fact that such a form of teaching, from his point of view, was, if anything, "worse" he replied, to the amusement of many people, that he was not taking his violin with him! What difference that made, he did not and, of course, could not say. It certainly could not mean that he was not going to demonstrate his way of playing on a different instrument. But his change of mind seems to me highly significant. It shows that there comes a point in time, when we all have to take a fresh look at old problems, regardless of previous personal convictions and experiences, however painful the memories and however unforgivable the actions which we are condemning.

Unnecessary to say that, of course, no plea in mitigation, let alone "defence" whatever of the German crimes is intended. There just isn't one. But, whether we like it or not, this has nothing to do with realistic factors and the way human nature works. Obviously, the attitude, especially of former refugees, cannot possibly be uniform. If you have lost a near relative or are even a holocaust survivor yourself, your feelings are bound to be different from those of people who have been spared such horrors.[39] There are matters we condemn, for want of a better word, on general, and others on personal grounds. The latter are far more compelling and, of course, apply to the bulk of refugees, whether regarding their own families' experiences or those of friends. This differing reaction is, as I said, human nature. To give an example in quite a different field: if we were to read in the paper that several thousand people in a far-off country were killed in the name of ethnic cleansing or whatever, we would naturally be indignant, disgusted, and condemn this crime in the strongest terms. But if we heard on the same day of a severe but non-fatal accident that happened to a neighbour of ours with whom we were merely on greeting terms, I venture to suggest that this would affect us emotionally more than the news of the thousands of innocent people slaughtered. The greater proximity of the event is one of the factors that decisively

---

[39] And this does not only seem to apply to former refugees. I remember from my job as an insurance broker that a Lloyd's underwriter refused to insure an aeroplane for no other reason than that it was the same type as that from which he had been shot down during the war.

matter. By the same token, former refugees are bound to be unforgiving for a longer period than other Jews. Yet, certain developments are inevitable even in their case, however unwelcome the recognition of this fact may be to us.

For about a decade after the war, feelings of forgiveness were unthinkable. What is more, Germany was genuinely regarded as a "non-country" – for practical purposes it did not exist. I personally experienced a significant example of this attitude: I was trying to find a publisher for my father's posthumous Memoirs, a book which, when it was eventually published, became a source work regarding musical, especially violinistic, life during the first half of the previous century; even today, there is hardly a musical dictionary which, when dealing with famous violinists of that period, will not quote from it. But for a long time I found it impossible to interest any British publisher, not least because the book had been written in German and would have had to be translated into English – something that would not have presented a problem of any size. What did not occur to me or to anybody else whose professional advice I sought, was the simple solution of approaching a German or even Swiss publisher. The idea of publishing anything in German, let alone doing business with Germany, simply did not occur to anybody; Germany was a non-country at the time and German a non-language.

Then, things began slowly to change. This for a number of practical reasons, with which, as far as German Jewish refugees are concerned, I have dealt in detail in my original treatment of this question[40] and need not repeat them here. What is of interest is to try and find a generally applicable reason for this change of attitude.

This is not really all that difficult; similar historical developments are all around us. Whilst, as we all know, German atrocities under the Nazis were in a class of their own, shameful acts committed by nations, their leaders and

---

[40] Ibid,

their citizens are legion. Leaving aside wars, we have had, in the past 2000 years, atrocities such as the treatment of slave gladiators and Christians in the Roman Empire; whose fate often depended on the whim of the emperor or spectators[41]; the burning of heretics and witches in the Middle Ages; the guillotining during the French revolution; the American lynchings; the public executions in this country, which were regarded as public entertainment; to name but a few. Seen from our cultural point of view today, they were all horrific. Yet, I cannot remember that, when we learned about them at school, any moral judgement was ever expressed. And there are people who dislike Frenchmen, Italians and Americans, but if asked for the reason, these atrocities will not be among those put forward. They are all in the past and have become "history", which can no longer affect us emotionally.

Alright, but this was hundreds and thousands of years ago. Yet what is unexpected is that this process does not have to take as long as in my examples– it can occur well within a life-time.[42] To put it another way – you cannot indefinitely hold against the next generation or generations the guilt of its forebears (though there is an exception for anti-Semites; "the Jews killed Jesus" is still one of their slogans). Hence, to cut a long story short, most former refugees recommenced, or a least did not actively object to, relations with Germany in one way or another as occasion arose; though of course neither forgetting nor forgiving the sins of the past. But this sentiment is, though there are exceptions, no longer directed against the present generation.

I myself had to deal with this problem when I joined, in

---

[41] Just think how thoughtlessly we use today the expression "thumbs down", quite forgetting that in former times the life of an unfortunate gladiator hinged on it.

[42] I am not alone in this opinion – vide Alan Bennett's play "The History Boys", which records a somewhat similar sentiment about the Holocaust, though, in that case, not on the part of a Jewish person.

.

the mid-1980s, i.e. 40 years after the collapse of Nazi Germany, a firm of Lloyd's Brokers with the task of extending that firm's German business. I decided to take a strong line from the outset. First meetings with German business contacts would usually take a predictable course. After 5 minutes, the German I was talking to would interrupt himself and exclaim: "I really must congratulate you on your excellent German! Where did you learn to speak it so well?" To which the obvious answer was "In Germany, until Hitler kicked me out as a Jew." I then waited for any adverse reaction, which would have meant the end of the meeting for me. It never came.

Of course, none of the people I met, mostly aged between 25 and 50, could have been Nazis, nor, so they told me, had their parents.[43] I felt, it would be best not to delve too deeply and to conduct, as it were, a cross examination, instead of taking the line of least resistance and accepting it except where it was blatantly untrue.

The stories told to prove such innocence would occasionally go to extraordinary lengths. One of my class-mates at prep school had been Hans Meissner, the son of the well-known German chef de cabinet since the revolution in 1918 who had managed to keep his job through all vicissitudes from Ebert to Hitler. When one day, I discovered in a bookshop a biography of, of all people, Magda Goebbels, the wife of the notorious Nazi propaganda minister, written by Hans Meissner, I managed to re-establish contact with him via his publishers. He stoutly maintained that his father had been a friend of the Jews all along and claimed that at his funeral an obviously Jewish man, whom he did not know, had put a large bunch of roses on his grave. Asked for the reason, he replied, according to Hans Meissner: "Every rose

---

[43] It reminds of the black joke: "How many Jews lived in Germany before Hitler came to power?" Answer: "40 million." "Don't be ridiculous!" "No, it is true. Every German claims to have saved the life of at least one of them."

represents the life of a Jew your father saved." The story was, in my opinion, almost certainly untrue and rather heavy-handed – but typical.[44]

People often ask why, if there were so many opponents of Hitler, the resistance did not play a larger part. Considering the danger to job, family, freedom and life, which even the slightest deviation from Nazism could trigger off, I feel that this lack of opposition is not surprising. The fact that resistance did exist, is well-documented, as are the extremely cruel ways of execution of those who were discovered.

I was once asked at a business luncheon in Germany: "You obviously like it here and have many friends. Why don't you come back to live in Germany?" This called for a frank answer; "Yes, I like it and I have made friends here. But nothing could ever induce me to move back to a country that committed these unspeakable crimes against members of my race." Apart from the inevitable answer "we are not the same" this was fully accepted.

Which brings me to the question, often neglected by commentators: How did the Germans feel towards us? When all is said and done, the bombings and destruction, killing, as they did, tens of thousands of civilians, many of whom must have been quite innocent, was barbaric from the German point of view, however necessary they were for winning the war. Interestingly enough, I never heard a direct complaint from a German about this. Most accepted the realities of war and, in many cases, the guilt that had made these actions

---

[44] Meissner, incidentally, told me an, as far as I know, little-known story (which I believe to be true, coming as it were, indirectly from the horse's mouth especially as there was no axe to grind. I think it is worth retelling if only because it shows that even Hitler could have his human side. There were, of course, constant intrigues by top people against one another and attacks on Meissner senior were no exception. On learning that Reichspräsident Hindenburg had died, Meissner is said to have burst into tears. This was promptly reported to Hitler as a sign of disloyalty to the Führer. But Hitler's reaction was unexpected: "What of it; I respect him for that".

necessary.

Not that every German realised the enormity of the crimes committed. I remember that, when I was looking for an additional employee in my business, one of the applicants turned out, at the interview, to be a former German prisoner of war, who, at the end of the conflict, had married an English girl and settled in this country. I told him gently that it would be quite impossible for me to employ him, since a large part of my clientele still consisted of former Jewish refugees and there might well be unpleasantness. He was puzzled: "But why? I had nothing against the Jews. I was always on friendly terms with them, until they were taken away." Precisely.

So, how can we sum up our attitude towards the Germany of today? I can do no better than repeat something written by the well-known journalist and writer Norman Lebrecht: "Not to forget, which would be unforgivable, nor even to forgive, which is a divine prerogative. But to found a new relationship with modern Germany, a multinational, multicultural society like our own, in which the past is a foreign country and the future will nourish a revivified Jewish community."

*

17

Suppressed music – a two-way traffic?

What is the question if the answer is "9 W"?

Well, you'll have to read on a little while until you get the answer (or, rather, the question). Meanwhile let us turn to what this section is about.

To coin a phrase, of all the art forms, music is unquestionably the most abstract. The majority of books and many paintings convey more or less concrete pictures, ideas, stories, opinions, subjects – in brief, anything that can be recognised and judged by our intellect as well as our feelings. We assess them according to our individual tastes, opinions and hang-ups as pleasing or not, or we find them interesting or uninteresting, skilful or amateurish, exciting or boring, or for some reason just not in tune with us. Whatever the case, we usually judge them on the basis of criteria that – subjective or objective, correct or incorrect – we can set out in a reasoned argument.

Our reaction to music, on the other hand – unless we are professional musicians or musicologists, and also disregarding our like or dislike of a specific more or less skilful interpreter – is governed overwhelmingly by our feelings, the abstract satisfaction or dissatisfaction we derive from it. It can also bother us because it is atonal (I am speaking here as a member of the older generation), played too loudly at an unsuitable venue (a restaurant, for instance) or out of hours. But it is very difficult to classify it as "objectionable" as such in the same way in which we do a book, play or painting (such as for instance, if you can describe it as a painting, that of Moira Hindley produced entirely by handprints of little children) which puts our back up or to which some of us may object because it is pornographic.

Is there any difference if a work consists of words set to music? Certainly not in the case of Lieder, but yes with songs of every description in which the music takes secondary place to the verbal sentiment expressed. We will reject, unhesitatingly and absolutely, the national-socialist Horst Wessel song, even in the unlikely event of our happening to like the tune; we would likewise hate a collection of Nazi songs, even in the inimitable style of Brahms' Festival Overture – a scenario as bizarre as unlikely. But apart from this, I can recall hardly any case in which music can be judged on anything but, well, just the music itself.

There are, of course, pieces where we like both words and music, as for instance Schumann's "Frauenliebe und Leben" or the "Rosenkavalier".

Other considerations apply to compositions without words that specifically celebrate or commemorate an historical event. We may approve of the sentiment, but if we do not like the music, the composer's good intentions come to naught.

Are operas in a different category? In those rare cases when they are pure propaganda for a certain political movement or opinion, they can cease to be "music" in its true sense and we are inclined and entitled to judge them by the afore-mentioned non-abstract criteria. But it is unquestionable that in any normal opera it is the music that matters, not the text or plot, which more often than not is very silly anyway.[45]

It is easy for authorities to give concrete reasons for the suppression (if the Law permits it) of a book, a play, an openly tendentious opera or even a painting. But this is not so for music in general; which, of course, did not and does not stop dictatorships from doing precisely that. We call it "suppressed music". When we refer to it we think, of course, in the first place of countries such as Stalin's Russia and

---

[45] It is possible, though; that we object so violently to a specific production of an opera that it spoils the music for us.

Hitler's Germany. The dictators did not necessarily dislike it, but in Russia it was the political orientation and in Germany the Jewish race of the composer that was the decisive factor. It goes without saying that this has nothing to do with the merits or demerits of a specific composition itself.

However, a country does not necessarily have to be a dictatorship to suppress music. Which brings us back to the initial"9 W" riddle: The question is: "Do you spell your name with a V, Herr Vagner?" "Nein, W." (Sorry, hardly worth waiting for.)

I am, of course, referring to the fact that Wagner's music is banned in Israel on account of his attitude towards Jews on the one hand and Hitler's attitude to him on the other. So much has been written about the question of whether his works should be performed there – or for that matter, to a lesser degree whether performances elsewhere should be attended by good Jews – that it is difficult to believe that anything new can be added. Well, perhaps not, but there is one aspect to which, as far as I know, little, if any, attention is being paid. I may be wrong, but I myself have never known the question of anti-Semitism to affect the homage we pay to immortal painters. Yet the countless depictions of religious themes, let alone those unflattering ones of Judas, make it reasonably certain that many of these artists must have had, *and expressed* anti-Semitic feelings and, as likely as not, quite strong ones. But no-one seems to suggest that their pictures should be shunned or banned for that reason. It is almost the same with writers unless they are really notorious for anti-Semitic or otherwise objectionable opinions. Hands up those who have ever given a thought to the question whether Michelangelo or Raphael liked or hated Jews. But why confine it to paintings and books? If Stradivarius had happened to be anti-Semitic, does this mean that no Israeli violinist or cellist ought to own a Strad? I have no idea about the views held about Jews by Rembrandt, Dürer, Monet, van Gogh and for that matter Stradivarius, and I daresay very few, if any, of my readers (art historians excepted) have either, but

I am sure that none of the Jewish art collectors or Jewish fiddlers, paying hundreds of thousands or more for one of their creations, ever even consider this aspect. And, of course, rightly so. The work of a genius, leaving aside its investment value, once created, stands entirely on its own merits. Then why is Wagner such an exception for Israel?

We all know that he was, by all accounts, a pretty unpleasant and utterly unscrupulous person and a convinced anti-Semite. He expressed his views freely, such as on the, in his view, pernicious Jewish influence on German art. To this opinion, however wrong, he was fully entitled. But, to my knowledge, he never advocated violence, and his operas hardly ever contain positive signs of anti-Semitism (a possible exception, Beckmesser in Die Meistersinger, is supposed to have been an attack on Hanslick, a Jewish musicologist and critic of the time, whom, however, Wagner disliked equally for reasons other than his race; and anyway, he did not advocate for Beckmesser to be murdered, but only to lose the girl he was after). Many of his operas have no political or racial overtones. We have, of course, the Ring, with its celebration of the German gods and heroes, to which, again, he was fully entitled. But he certainly did not spare them as far as his depiction of their characters was concerned. On the contrary, they were really all a pretty frightful bunch and I would have hated to meet any of them in a dark alley.

Then why, I repeat, all this emotion just about Vagner – sorry, Wagner? It certainly cannot be his personality. Picasso had, from what one reads, an equally unsavoury character, but nobody refuses to exhibit his paintings on these grounds, and, as far as I know, Mahler's works are being performed in Israel, though he converted to Christianity purely for reasons of personal advancement – not exactly a Brownie point in Jewish eyes.

The reason for singling out Wagner is, of course, that Hitler "adopted" him, made him, as it were, an honorary Nazi and indeed one of the – if I may be allowed this word – cultural pillars of the Nazi creed. This was without Wagner's knowledge or consent. Yes, it is of course, practically certain that, had he lived during the Nazi period, he would have loved it and have been an ardent *Parteigenosse*, but he didn't and so he wasn't, though his family certainly were. We can blame him for the Nazi crimes as little as we can other Germans who were not alive during the time of the Holocaust, though, let us face it, not a few of them – however violently they will deny it today – might well have been infected by the virus. Committing a crime is something you do, not something you think. Most of us have little or no hesitation in communicating with those Germans who were lucky enough to be born after Hitler's reign, (I am writing about it in another context in this book). So why should we treat people who lived and died before him differently? Wagner was entitled to his anti-Jewish opinions as well as his pro-Germanic sentiments and his glorification of German gods, however we may dislike them, as long as they remained just opinions or products of his imagination. In brief, I can see no logical reason why he should be regarded as a special case compared with all the other anti-Semitic geniuses and potential Nazis who lived before the Hitler period.

Needless to say, this is not intended as a defence of Wagner the man; and even less his opinions (though, as a matter of fact, his recommended remedy against the alleged Jewish influence on German music was assimilation, not destruction). But they ought not to matter. No-one can deny that he was a genius and that his operas, whether we happen to like them or not, enriched the world and continue to do so. It is worth repeating: a work of art, once completed, stands by itself and is entirely detached from its creator. His character, his behaviour, his opinions are simply not relevant as long as what they represent is not objectionable on general grounds. Boycotting the works of a genius for non-artistic reasons is entirely unjustified and smacks of cultural dictatorship, whether the composers name is Wagner or Mendelssohn.

I will mention only in passing that in Wagner's case it seems that the opinion of many members of the Israeli population varies from that of its rulers – vide the number of Israelis who visit Bayreuth every year if they are lucky enough to have obtained tickets, that is.

What if Wagner had lived during the Hitler period? His works would still have been those of a genius, but would the arguments I have put forward be invalidated, since the time scale has changed and he would doubtless have lapped up National Socialism? If this had been so, many of us would find it very difficult to *stomach* him. But he would still have been the genius he was, which would be more important than his objectionable opinions.

Hitler was a professional painter, by all accounts a very mediocre one, but let us assume for the sake of argument that he had been one of genius. Could any Jew possess a painting by him? Should the rule that a work, once produced, is separated from its producer, not apply to him, as well? The answer is No, because there is this decisive difference: Hitler was able to put his theories into practice with catastrophic results that caused death and unspeakable suffering to millions. In such a blatant case the misdeeds outweigh any other consideration: everything he did would be tainted. But the same can certainly not be said of Wagner. Many Nazis no doubt admired him simply because Hitler did, but I am certain that his music did not cause one additional Holocaust death.

However, let us not forget the time scale. Suppose, if I may be allowed to put up this impossible case, King Herod had been a painter of genius and some of his works still existed. In that case the negative factors would be by no means as decisive as in the case of Hitler, because we are now dealing with "history", which is no longer governed by subjective emotions. There is no good reason why this should be so, except the lapse of time.

Seen from that angle, it is not unthinkable that, one day, Wagner's music will again become acceptable in Israel simply because he lived so long ago. An intriguing question: Will it still be regarded as a work of genius or will he be dated and be simply a historical curiosity? Unthinkable for Wagner fans of the present time, but how immortal is immortal, really?

*

18

Adultery, is it…?

"Thou shalt not admit adultery."

Schoolboy howler.

Is it *what*? I could have chosen any word or words to complete this question – wrong, pleasant, risky, inevitable, desirable. alright for some, forbidden under any circumstances, best to be avoided, good for preserving a marriage, fatal for it, etc. etc. But I am not qualified to write about this question, as I have no more experience than the average amateur, nor am I up-to-date with statistics about unfaithful husbands, wives or partners, quite apart from the fact that, for obvious reasons, any information they give is likely to be suspect anyway. What originally triggered off these musings, were two stories concerning former prime ministers: (a) the revelation some time in 2003, that, a long time ago, John Major had bedded Mrs Edwina Curry, and (b) yet another biography of Harold Wilson supposed to throw fresh light on his mysterious relationship with his secretary, Lady Marcia Falconer.

What intrigues me is the ambivalence and inconsistency shown by most people when these matters come up. It seems OK for film, pop, TV, football (with exceptions) and similar stars, as well as writers and painters to have boy and girl friends of different or the same sex, to change them frequently and to show off their latest acquisition to an admiring public. This sort of news will fill the tabloids ad nauseam. The papers will also occasionally go into the effect on the marriages, if any, of the people involved. But the question whether this behaviour is moral or immoral is hardly ever raised. Frequent changes of sexual partners seem to be regarded almost as a birthright of these people. But let a politician stray from the marital path, the opposite rules apply and moral indignation is almost automatic. It seems to be different in France, where during our now almost-forgotten Profumo scandal the French prime minister of the time is said famously to have observed that, if he were to take any notice of matters like that, he would never be able to complete his cabinet.

The public's attitude is all the more remarkable as politicians are held in low esteem by a great many people. Lying (except "to the House", an unforgivable crime if they get found out[46]), broken promises and lack of morals in general – if they don't amount to the buzzword "sleaze" (whatever the difference may be) are regarded as almost par for the course. So why marital infidelities should be regarded so differently, why the "offenders" should suddenly become lapsed role models of propriety is somewhat of a mystery, at least to me. True, most politicians talk about family values, back to basics and similar high-falutin matters, but this does not necessarily mean that they are insincere if they themselves occasionally deviate from the principles they proclaim.

There are two points that should be made.

The first is the undoubted fact that adultery does not automatically wreck a marriage, or else there would not be very many married couples left. Married men or women who stray from the marital path, usually need to satisfy an urge which is in most of us, namely that for sexual variety (vide the schoolboy howler: "In Western countries marriage is possible only to one partner. It is called monotony"). But the unfaithful spouses do not necessarily have to be emotionally involved outside marriage, and basic loyalty to the spouse, partner and the children – in brief the much-vaunted "family

---

[46] A new "crime – seems to have been added recently. The shadow art minister Boris Johnson who had had an extra-marital affair, lost his job, because he lied about it to his party leader. Press and public seem to have swallowed this reason without realising how absurd it is. Scout's honour!

values" – remain unaffected more often than not. As is well-known, being occasionally unfaithful is regarded by not a few people as a kind of safety valve in the marriage, preventing, in the last resort, its breakdown. Those who do not succumb to temptation of this kind, admit very rarely to experiencing it. Wisely: a well-known exception was the former American president Jimmy Carter who during his election campaign was rash enough to declare that during his marriage he had not infrequently been lusting after other women (apparently without doing anything about it). And where did it get him? Into the distinct danger of wrecking his election chances.

Unrelieved sexual urges can be very troublesome and their suppression can require a lot of mental energy. A minister of state has enormous responsibilities requiring all the energy he can muster. Is it worthwhile to expend part of it on a matter which could be dealt with so easily (and pleasurably) in other ways? Nobody will grudge him the occasional round of golf "to recharge his batteries". It is not "news". I know I am saying something politically wholly incorrect, but why not treat discreet (discreet!) extra-marital sex in the same way by simply ignoring it and not making it "news"? I am putting this point without intending to be flippant, I really mean it. I would also like to ask the morally indignant whether they are certain they have the right to cast the first stone.

Which brings me to the second point. If we ourselves do or take part in something we normally regard as morally wrong, our attitude may be different from that we adopt if the same act is committed by others. Hands up those who can honestly disagree with that! I myself can't: I remember in my younger years – and please note, well before my marriage – having a girl friend who, on returning from a fortnight's holiday at her parental home, confessed to me that she had got engaged to the son of family friends. Obviously, our relationship had to be at an end. "But", she added somewhat matter-of factly, "let us go to bed just once more for old time's sake." As it happened, I had myself been on the verge of finishing the relationship (she just had beaten me to it), hence I was anything but upset, but in fact rather relieved by the way the problem had resolved itself. However, it occurred to me that her suggestion was highly immoral for a newly engaged young girl (who could not possibly yet be bored with her partner), and that I certainly would not have liked to be in the shoes of her fiancé. In fact I found her attitude very wrong indeed. But then I thought "Ah, well, it's only me, so it's OK" and I gave the moral question no further thought. Clearly, the fact that it was "only me" wasn't anything like a good reason for consenting to something that I had been disapproving of in principle, and if I had been asked for my opinion about a similar attitude by somebody else, I would have condemned it. But it shows that considering something to be wrong and then doing that very same thing ourselves, does not necessarily make us hypocrites. For we instinctively regard ourselves as a special case. We all have urges to which the majority of us succumb from time to time. It does not necessarily mean that it is dishonest for us to preach the right thing, as long as we do not turn it into a moral crusade, strongly condemning or even persecuting the wrongdoers. Somerset Maugham has dealt with the syndrome very neatly in his short story "The Rains Came" I feel that the young married priest in that story who repeatedly prayed with a prostitute in order to reform her, but was eventually unable himself to resist what he felt were his baser instincts, and "had his way with her", as it is so nicely expressed, was definitely over-reacting by committing suicide.

What does matter, in my opinion, is whether we allow our real duties and responsibilities towards job and family to be affected by the "wrong" we are doing, such as it is. John Major clearly did not, or else he would not have refused Mrs. Currie the ministerial post she apparently craved. In this respect, he behaved impeccably, a sign, incidentally, that he was not emotionally involved or at least not greatly so. I don't know whether it is true that his own marriage had been beginning to crumble, but if so, the event may have been the catalyst that brought it back on to an even keel. The one point, on which he blew it for me, was that he felt obliged to say that the episode was the thing he had been most ashamed of in his whole life. Come off it, John! It seems that politicians can't live without committing hypocrisy of the worst kind. I am sure he enjoyed every minute of it, or else he would have stopped; Mrs. C. was, after all, an attractive lady at the time, notwithstanding Lady Archer's subsequent bitchy comment to the effect that his taste was the only thing John Major had to be ashamed of.

Harold Wilson's case was much more serious – he really seems sometimes to have been influenced in his political behaviour and decisions by his attachment. Incidentally, it is maintained by many people that there was no consummated sexual relationship. If this is correct, it is an open question whether it might not have been better for his freedom of thought and judgement if there had been. It seems to prove my point re misdirected energy. I have no knowledge of it, but I have no doubt that it must have been a strain on his marriage. Yet, as far as I remember, he got much less stick from public and press than Mr Major.

The recent case of our former Home Secretary David Blunkett is interesting from yet some other points of view. His affair with a married woman was rightly regarded as a private matter, but his "offence" was that he was said to have abused his position and, inter alia, to have speeded up the decision on a residence application of his lover's children's nanny, the granting of which would apparently have been a foregone conclusion anyway. To me this seems an extraordinarily flimsy reason. I believe it is on a par with a butcher saving his best joint for a favourite customer; an overworked plumber dealing with a friend's emergency out of turn; a doctor making a home visit which he would not have made if the patient had not happened to be a personal friend; or even Mr Blair not having to queue at the airport like ordinary people when going on holiday. Social life could not function without these occasional kindnesses and privileges, which do not disadvantage anyone.[47] If Mr. Blunkett had admitted what he had done from the outset, adding that he did not regard this as a resigning matter, I am sure he would still be in office. It is the hypocritical attitude of our politicians who want to show, against all the evidence, that they are whiter than white – sorry! cleaner than clean – that brought about his downfall, and rightly so. Anyway, resignations for such reasons seem now-a-days to be a purely temporary affair. How is that for hypocrisy?

By the same token I remain convinced that, if Mr Profumo at the time had maintained that his sex life was his private affair as long as it did not affect his job, he would not have had to "lie to the House" and not have had to resign. Of course, the girl in question had a simultaneous affair with a Russian diplomat, but the suggestion that this represented a risk to security – indiscrete pillow talk between a minister of State and a call girl, I ask you! – is really too silly to be entertained. It only shows up the naivety and unworldliness of the people who expressed this ludicrous suspicion in all seriousness.

It seems to be a fact that the less seriously the politicians involved take these matters, the less they are remarked upon. The prime example for this was, of course, the late Alan Clark, a former minister of State, whose Diaries, in which he told all, became a bestseller. They did not produce an adverse reaction on the part of the public, but on the contrary just good-humoured indulgence. This surely proves the point of the subsequent behaviour of the "culprit" being of major importance.

The motives of the lady in the case who "tells all" are another matter. As far as they are financial, they are beneath contempt. But often it may be simply a case of the "woman

---

[47] One might even say that they are built into our system. If an MP helps a constituent in some way, who can doubt that, the complaint will receive special treatment and be dealt with more quickly than the same one by a constituent who did not approach his MP? This is what, inter alia, MPs are for.

scorned" in one way or another. The best example for that is that of Cecil Parkinson; I feel certain that he or rather Mrs. Thatcher could have handled the matter better. What he did, after all, was to stick to his wife instead of his girl friend, surely a decision we should approve of. Yet in his case that did not help him .It seems remarkable that in many instances the woman in the case, even if she is married herself, escapes censure. The whims of public opinion or rather the press treatment that creates it are an enduring mystery.

The most striking case is, of course, that of the late Princess Diana and Prince Charles, where again the guilt in the public mind was distinctly that of Charles. The matter has been flogged to near-death – "near" because the public and the press won't let it die – so often that no useful purpose would be served by doing it yet again. But it does underline the grave consequences of these matters being mishandled by one party involved taking the wrong attitude from the outset.

As I said in the beginning, I have no answer to the question in the title. But there are hidden contradictions and riddles here that ought to be examined in a way less narrow-minded and prejudiced than commonly happens today.

19

Class and the subconscious mind – any connection?

> *"The mark of an educated mind is to be able to entertain an idea without accepting it."*
>
> Aristotle

When, many years ago, I saw the TV broadcast of the moon landing and pictures of the earth, which, surprise, surprise, turned indeed out to be round for all to see, someone who was watching with me said "This is the end of the Flat Earth Society". However, I have been told that it still exists, albeit with a severely curtailed membership. What is it that makes people cling to a belief that is so obviously wrong? I don't know but I am beginning to wonder whether I am one of them: the theory I am about to develop, has to my knowledge not been *proved* wrong, but has been derided by practically everybody to whom I have tried to explain it. In fact, it was the occasion I mentioned in my foreword, when one Mensa member called me (a co-member!) "stupid". Is this a record?

The piece which I am reprinting here in a somewhat amended form was an article which I had originally written for the British Mensa Newsletter. Part of it had aroused considerable and incredulous hilarity in my own family and the rage and ridicule of various correspondents to the journal. Having reread it, I find it just as valid as I had then, hence I am resuscitating it. In my defence, I might add that, at the time, it had been the co-founder of Mensa, the great Victor Serebriakoff himself, on the occasion of my showing him round Lloyd's, who had encouraged me to publish my ideas in his magazine. With hindsight I am wondering whether I may have overlooked his tongue firmly planted in his cheek.[48]

My contention at the time was (1) that the much-advertised classless society is an impossibility and (2) that the average person (needless to say, there are exceptions) makes subconscious efforts not to change into a higher, but to remain in his/her original class. (Incidentally, I touched on this theme in my book "Where do you come from," but since I referred in that context mainly to Middle-European refugees from the Nazi regime, it does not cover the whole problem.) What exposed me to particular ridicule at the time were not my opinions on this particular subject, but my conclusion resulting therefrom about the occasional – I repeat, occasional – motivation of strikes. Wait for it.

Let us take the classless argument first. Class can be defined as a group of people in similar social, occupational and economic circumstances sharing by and large certain cultural and behavioural characteristics and patterns. Today, at least on the face of it, this is no longer entirely correct, as far as the financial side is concerned – vide pop stars, footballers' et al, many having originated in the working class, earning enormous sums of money, attracting millions of fans, acquiring cult status and thus running counter to the accepted economic and social patterns. However, in not a few cases this is a passing phase – many, for a variety of reasons, after their heydays, sink back into comparative poverty and obscurity. As a matter of fact, I believe that their fate in some cases supports my opinion – to which I am coming later – about our desire to stick to our original class. However, for

---

[48] Well, actually, this does not seem to be the case after all. I have found a letter from him in which he refers to my "fascinating article" and continues: "I note with amused interest that your opponents seem to be quite incapable of argument without resorting to *argumentum ad hominem*. Oddly enough they seem to think that this enhances their case. I suppose it was Marx himself who started the fashion..." (which was news to me). Anyway, however wrong my opinions may be, I feel that with this testimony I don't have to hide them under a bushel.

the purpose of my argument, I am going to disregard these people as non-typical, interesting though their cases sometimes are.

It is obvious that any society is bound to consist of individuals with widely differing skills, knowledge, cultural interests, assets and social aspirations. For such a complex conglomeration to be dumped into the same mould, i.e., being "classless" in accordance with the accepted definition of class, is neither possible nor, I suggest, desirable. I am, of course, conscious of the fact that the class system is attacked in the first place on account of being unfair, based as it so often is, on birth, unearned wealth and undeserved privilege. That this is a considerable flaw, causing many reformers to strive for a change, is well known and, from their point of view, laudable. But the question is: whether possible or not, would a change really be desirable? Could anything better be put in its place? I don't believe so. True, it would probably do justice to some people disadvantaged under the present system, but at the same time it would if it were achievable (which it isn't) be far less fair to a different and probably much larger set of people, as I shall try to show. Thus it would be as broad as it is long or one might even say, broader than long.

Ideally, everybody ought to have the same start in life, eventually attaining the position to which they are entitled on "merit". But there is no doubt that people's mental equipment differs widely, not only in intelligence but also in leadership potential and other respects. In order to avoid waste, our educational system would obviously have to be adapted accordingly; it would be highly inefficient to give the Einstein treatment to someone capable only of doing a menial job. Hence, differentiations would have to be made from the outset. But how, in practice, could we give to everybody the *correct* start suiting their particular abilities? And who would be competent and have the necessary authority to judge these merits/demerits and determine the category and educational and social streams into which an individual should be placed at an early age? And how could this possibly be achieved without in many cases disrupting family life? And what indeed should be the standard applied – IQ, character, physical attributes, inherited genes or what? At what stage in life should the decision be made? What about late developers? What if the assessment turns out to have been faulty or is regarded as such by the parties concerned – would there be the possibility of an appeal against it? And how would we go about directing everybody into the class that is right for them, without falling foul of Human Rights legislation and causing, as already indicated, havoc in the circle of the family? What would be the feelings of those and their nearest and dearest who, rightly or wrongly, have been found officially to be inferior to their parents, siblings, friends? How would the brain surgeon feel whose son is incapable of doing anything more qualified than an unskilled labourer's job, and vice versa? What would be the feelings of the "inferior" person?

With all these inevitable personal difficulties, what about all the psychological and other problems arising for all parties involved? The number of psychotherapists would have to be doubled or trebled to satisfy the demand. As already indicated, it would not necessarily have to be only a case of inferiority. If a child were to be judged to be very much superior to the parents, what then? If the family are assessed as being incapable of doing it justice, should it be removed and placed in more propitious surroundings? This list is anything but exhaustive. The problems that would ensue would be as unmanageable as they would be endless.

We can see some of them in the form of Tony Blair's Labour Government encouraging as many people as possible to become university students. What a clumsy, inefficient and costly method of separating (or, rather, not separating) the wheat from the chaff! Quite a number of students drop out after a comparatively short time and, one hopes, are not too discouraged to take up one of the more congenial and by no means inferior occupations. And what the present scheme, in my view, has not fully considered either, is the "more-chiefs-than-indians' syndrome, i.e., the question whether there will be sufficient jobs suitable for those highly qualified people who have completed their studies. The difficulty for a fully trained graduate to find a congenial job or *any* job (because it is a frequent experience of such people that they are regarded as overqualified and therefore unsuitable for the job on offer) is a very real one and can cause an enormous amount of unhappiness and frustration. *Cui bono*?

Obviously, the system, if it were practicable at all (which, I think I have succeeded in showing it is not) would not only be as unfair as the present haphazard one, albeit for different reasons and to a different set of people, but it would cause a great deal more administrative work, confusion and unhappiness than the current non-selection situation. For all its flaws, the present one works. "If it ain't broke, don't fix it".

To come to the second point I want to make: basically, and, to repeat, of course with many exceptions – most of us are, in spite of a sometimes voiced opinion to the contrary, not really particularly unhappy in the position into which we have been placed by the accident of birth, fate or whatever. And not only are we relatively content, I make bold to assert that we even strive actively to maintain this position in which we feel by and large so comfortable. On the other hand, of course, nobody wants to sink into a lower class.

That this is the general tendency, can be seen from the example of the average Middle-European Jewish refugee who had to leave his country in the 1930s and settled in Great Britain. A goodish proportion were young, some middle-aged, often penniless, with no job to go to, no prospects, no connections and with language difficulties to boot. Most of them had the same start at the bottom of the ladder and although they were often forced to follow paths very different from those they had been treading at home, lo and behold, within a comparatively short time the majority, young or old, originally rich or poor, (yes, I know, again with notable, not to say sensational exceptions in either direction) found their way back to, homed in as it were, on the same occupation, income and life style, in other words, class to which they had belonged or for which they had been destined at home. And I firmly believe that the same would apply to the population generally; why should refugees be an exception?

Let me emphasise here that what we are dealing with is mainly a subconscious state of mind. As I said, the majority of us are satisfied with what and where we are and rarely give the matter any prolonged conscious thought. There is, indeed, no reason why we should: on the whole, the question whether we are successful or a failure in what we do, will be judged by comparison with people in the same category as ourselves. A factory foreman will not compare himself with a brain surgeon, but with his colleagues at work. It follows that success or failure will usually not affect our class membership.

But I will go further than that and maintain that we actively tend to resist change. I for one would feel quite unhappy if I were suddenly to be "promoted" into the class of landed gentry or multi-millionaires (which does not mean that I would not like to have the money!) Yes, there are people who, often with surprising success, consciously strive to better themselves and succeed in attaining membership of a "higher" class. But they are the exceptions that prove the rule.

It might, of course, be maintained, that this does not apply equally, and that members of the working class are generally less satisfied with their lot than others; after all, they often say so. I don't agree. From what I saw during my war work as an unskilled labourer in a factory, most workers whatever they may say to the contrary, are not unhappy with their position. They were conditioned to their life style from birth, and very probably would not feel comfortable elsewhere.

Now I want to go yet a step further and talk about *strikes,* but before I do so, let me make a few simple points to set the scene.

1. I think it can be accepted that as a general rule a strike as such means, short-term, a financial loss for the striker. Of course, in many cases he or she will be supported by their Union as well as the State; in addition, on resumption of work, they may be doing overtime and make good part if not all of their losses in this way. But basically, it will have cost them some money. The subsequent gain, if any, arises from the success, if any, which the strike action has achieved.

2. This will normally consist of higher wages, improved pensions, more paid holidays or better working conditions. But the actual gain of a successful strike may in fact not be very marked and often be quite long-term, i.e., it may take a comparatively long time for the financial improvement to make up the loss suffered in the first place. Let us visualise a dispute in which the difference between the employers' offer and the employees' demands is as little as 10% of the total wage. Let us further assume an hourly rate of £10, which for a 40 hour week means £400 p.w. The differential is thus £40 per week. If the strike lasts one week, the loss to the worker will take 10 weeks to make good, two weeks 20 weeks and so on, reduced though by the benefits received from other sources. Hence, striking does not necessarily have to be a particularly favourable economic proposition. Yet strikes are called for even smaller demands and for lesser, often scurrilous reasons such as the length of a tea break, the positioning of a stove, finding a dead rat in the loo, and so on.

3. There can be no doubt that many strikes, especially the wild-cat ones just mentioned, could have been avoided by negotiation.

4. The Union's decision and order to strike is almost invariably followed immediately and without being questioned.

5. It is a well-known fact that some people and in particular manual workers who have happened to earn a lot of overtime, decide, instead of keeping their gain, to take some time off, losing a certain amount of regular wages, thereby bringing their income back to its normal level.

Now back to my theory. It is in two parts: (a) Working people are no exception to subconsciously striving to stay in their own class and (b) some (but, of course, it cannot be repeated sufficiently often, by no means all) strikes can be one of the means by which this can be achieved.

(a) Workers are, or are supposed to be proud of belonging to the working class. But actually there are two working classes: skilled and unskilled. The distinction is very important to the skilled ones: on the one hand it is the justified pride in the skill itself, on the other the wish not to be regarded as akin to the lower, the unskilled, working class. For the latter reason they are extremely jealous of the well-known financial "differentials" that distinguish them from the unskilled worker. They will go to any length to maintain them. There is, of course, no reason why they shouldn't, but it shows in my opinion that finance, i.e., the actual income bracket, plays a greater part in the worker's class definition than it does for members of other classes. As an anecdotal example let me cite the words uttered some time ago by no lesser a person than the deputy Prime Minister John Prescott who declared: "We are all middle-class now." This silly and for a prominent socialist curiously inept remark can have referred only to improved financial conditions as opposed to social position or cultural interests or pursuits. I doubt, incidentally, that the working class was particularly impressed by this remark. Or take the case of a member of the working class winning the pools or the lottery. (I do not intend to sound snobbish, but workers seem to be the only people ever to win those prizes). Ten to one they will declare that this will not make any difference to their choice of friends. Members of other classes would not think, certainly not in the first place, of the possibility of changing their social circle on account of sudden wealth: for them, economic factors play a smaller part in the question of their class consciousness. A university lecturer with a modest income does not consider himself below a plumber although the latter probably enjoys considerably higher earnings (and may also be doing work more useful to society at large).

Another typical example. One day, during my war work as an unskilled labourer, a splinter got lodged below my nail, a somewhat painful experience. "Let me look at it", one of my colleagues, the leader of my section, said. To my horror, he produced a very dirty and rusty pocket knife and removed the object without causing me any pain or discomfort whatever. I was astounded. "You should have become a surgeon!" I exclaimed admiringly. "Well, I considered it, but then I thought "Why bother". I am sure this man would have been highly pleased to be promoted to foreman, but a surgeon – no; it would have taken him out of his class, something he obviously did not care for.

(b) If my above conclusions are tenable, i.e., that the money bracket plays a very important part in the class consciousness of workers and that they, like everybody else, tend to make subconscious efforts to remain in their own class – what follows? Clearly, should the possibility of an upward change of class appear on the horizon, they will take steps to avoid it. And since the change is usually expressed in earning so much more money that it might take them out of their class, they must find ways to resist *that*. A, for want of a better word, hand to mouth existence in the sense of usually not making anything like sufficient provision for the future, is part of their class culture. And how do you earn less money?

By working less. And how can you achieve that? By taking time off. But habitually just working fewer hours is not on. You may achieve it by faking illness or disability, but this is, in the long run, not an efficient method and anyway, there is certainly no reason to suppose that members of the working class are less honest in this respect than members of others. What is the alternative method? Strikes, which, as I have demonstrated, mean a short-term loss of income.

Yes, here we have it: I do believe that some strikes are caused by the subconscious wish of the striker NOT to earn more money than at present. Clearly, nobody in their right mind, in whatever class, will, unless he is a hopeless idealist, *consciously* wish to reduce their income or avoid earning a higher one. Even less will he admit to it or take any conscious steps to this end. He must have a different, legitimate reason. Remember, we are dealing, in the resistance to change, not with conscious but with subconscious motivations. If more income could mean the possible and subconsciously unwelcome loss of working class status, then conscious and subconscious desires are in conflict and ways must be found to make it possible for them to co-exist. There are good examples in other areas for this to be possible. We have only to think of permanent invalids or semi-invalids. The majority are, of course, genuine, but for others it can be nothing more than the well-known "flight into illness" enabling them to avoid having to face reality. But if you were to suggest this to them, they would indignantly deny it. And, of course, in a way they are right: most of them wish consciously nothing better than to regain their health and strength; it is only their subconscious motivation that makes them cling to their symptoms. Today, it is an accepted fact by the followers of psychoanalysis that our conscious and our subconscious wishes can be diametrically different from one another. Unbeknown to us, those in our subconscious may prove to be the stronger ones, and we therefore act to satisfy them without in the least realising that we are doing it. I can see no reason why this should not equally be so for some (I repeat again, some) strikes, i.e. those for which a reasonable economic justification is sometimes difficult, if not downright impossible to find and the objectives of which, such as they are, could be achieved much more effectively by other means.

As I said in the beginning, our union system imposes a very strong discipline on its members, but I believe that this is only possible because and as long as it corresponds to the subconscious wishes of members themselves. It is a well-known fact that, if a strike lasts too long and the financial hardships begin to bite, strikers will start drifting back, because consciously they cannot afford to stay out any longer and subconsciously because they are satisfied that the "danger" of having a surfeit of money has been averted. And don't put too much weight on sympathy strikes either. Some are genuine; others may be motivated by a convenient opportunity to satisfy pre-existing subconscious wishes.

It cannot be repeated too often that there are, without question, a great many strikes that are started on tenable grounds; whether justified or not is not at issue here. But I see no reason why this has to mean that *all* strikes are motivated in this way. In my opinion, subconscious factors sometimes play a decisive part. I believe that if the famous "man from Mars" came to this earth and looked at the position, he would not find this opinion strange, seeing the ludicrous reasons or rather excuses for some cessation of work.

So much for strikes. To return briefly to the pop stars, footballers' *et al* with working class origins who earn unbelievable riches for some period and, when their time has passed, sink back into poverty because they have wasted their money in unbelievably irresponsible ways. Who can say that their subconscious motive is sometimes not a simple desire to rejoin their class?

Think about it!

20

Paedophilia.

*"My own belief is that there is hardly anyone whose
sex life, if it were broadcast, would not fill the
world at large with surprise and horror."*

W. Somerset Maughan

This is a very difficult subject to write about, because if you say anything deviating in the slightest from the general contempt and loathing of paedophiles, you are apt to be completely misunderstood and even accused of defending them. So, let me begin by stating unequivocally, that, of course, active paedophilia is a crime that has to be punished. There are no two ways about it.

Is there anything more to be said? I believe there is – not least about the extremely violent reaction this crime almost invariably arouses. It is well-known that imprisoned paedophiles are often in danger of assault by fellow prisoners who may be morally quite depraved in other respects. Some may, in fact have themselves mistreated or abandoned their children and got away with it. Is this reaction really always in keeping with the severity of the crime or could it sometimes be out of proportion? Might there be cases in which the damaging effects are less severe than is so generally supposed? For that matter, what about the paedophiles themselves? Is it correct to lump them all together or are there differences between them?

Judging by the outraged reaction of people with whom I have discussed this matter, it seemed to me sometimes that there must be something wrong with me in even raising these questions. Was I really quite alone? No. The well-known prison doctor, writer and journalist Theodore Dalrymple, in an article in the "New Statesman" some time ago, called the fear of paedophilia exaggerated and the reaction hysterical. I admit that I cannot follow some of his reasoning, and the heading of his article "A Nation of Paedophiles" goes way over the top. But in other ways he does make sense. Be that as it may, why not look at the problem in a less emotional and more balanced frame of mind?

After all, the public do tend from time to time to over-react. And attitudes change. Take smoking. There is no doubt that it can be highly damaging to the health of the smoker. That, of course, is his or her own affair. But it can also be damaging to others: passive smoking. However, there is no doubt that some of the noxious fumes we inhale daily in the street without complaining or indeed giving them a thought are just as bad for *us all* and not only the comparatively few who have to endure passive smoking. Might therefore walking in the street, in not a few cases, have the effect often attributed to passive smoking? I have not heard of any agitation to ban motor cars for that reason. Those of us, who are old enough, know that 40 – 50 years ago smoking was a fully accepted social custom. Not to have a box of cigarettes at the disposal of one's guests was bad form. Offering one to someone you met, was almost automatic. If, in a crowded cinema one of the actors on the screen lit a cigarette, within ten seconds hundreds of lighters would blink in the audience. And indeed there can be no doubt that smoking can be a useful palliative preventing other things that can also be damaging or antisocial. Today we are better informed about the health risks than in former times. But is this a reason for some people to regard smokers almost as pariahs? The balanced view, where has it gone? I should perhaps add that I myself gave up smoking a great many years ago and did my best successfully, I am glad to say, to prevent my children from acquiring the habit. But in my house, any visitor can smoke as long as none of the other guests object. And there have been no ill-effects to anybody, nor do I expect any.

Nowadays we are treating drug addicts with far more

tolerance than smokers. You say the difference is that they can't do damage to others? What about the accidents under the influence of drugs, and the muggers who take to violent crime in order to support their craving? Not to forget the fact that long-term drug takers tend to become a dead loss and a burden on society.

Drunkenness, of course, is another "evil". But people who drink to excess are usually looked at with comparative indulgence, though they do quite enough damage – drunken driving accounts for many lives. Who knows, in 25 years' time a case may be made against drinking, resulting in it being regarded in much the same light as smoking is today. Stranger things have happened. Public opinion is fickle, unpredictable and certainly often far from correct.

But back to paedophilia. Let us start with the definition. Basically, a paedophile is a person, usually a male, who is sexually attracted to and aroused by children. Well, as it happens, the overwhelming majority of us are attracted to and aroused by mature though frequently quite young people of the opposite or the same sex as the case may be. This in itself is, to my best knowledge and belief, not a punishable offence or else 90% of the population would be permanently in prison with not enough prison warders to go round. Obviously there is nothing wrong with being sexually aroused by anybody or, for that matter, anything, but the point is, of course, whether or not one gives way to that urge in an improper manner. But here we come to the factor that distinguishes paedophiles from other people with sexual urges: the latter are permitted, more and more, subject, by the way, to certain extremely flexible, complicated and by no means unanimously agreed rules, actively "to do something" about it if they go about it in the "correct" way, whereas the paedophile is not, because for him there is no "proper" way of gratification. Quite rightly so, but, clearly, this may make things very difficult for him. If he remains a law abiding citizen, he may become very frustrated. Well, that's just too bad for him, but we, the public, sense this dilemma and the added temptation it brings, and for that reason are apt to suspect the worst.

Let us be clear about one thing: if the offence degenerates into violence, it ceases to be paedophilia and becomes rape, torture or even murder, quite irrespective of the perpetrator's specific sexual inclinations. There is, to my knowledge, no evidence leading to the belief that there are more sadists and murderers among paedophiles than among normal hetero- and homosexuals. The former just get more coverage in the press and are therefore more easily identified with capital crimes in the public mind. But to my knowledge there is no real basis to support this.

It is tempting to draw a parallel between paedophiles and catholic priests, in that both are forbidden to act out their sexual urges. But whilst paedophiles have to abstain willy-nilly, catholic priests chose this restricted way of life voluntarily, though I am not convinced that they always do so for spiritual reasons; it may well be a "legitimate" and initially satisfying way out for some who are sexually inadequate, inhibited or who are – at least in their own eyes – abnormal. I don't know whether there are reliable (or any known) statistics of how many of them break their vow of chastity, but unfortunately we hear quite often of cases where they do so by sexually molesting children. Unless they had these criminal tendencies from the outset – unlikely with men of the cloth – they must regard paedophilia as the lesser offence against their religious obligations or else they would presumably resort to normal sexual behaviour. A fascinating thought this: in some eyes and by no means those at the lowest level of society paedophilia seems to be regarded as the lesser offence than normal sexual conduct. Entirely misguided, of course, but there it is, for us to ponder about.

Basically I know of no particular reason why a paedophile's sexual urges should be stronger – and therefore less easy to control – than those of other people. The difference, as I already said, lies in the absolute taboo to following their inclinations. I don't know whether "inclination" is the right word. In some cases, "nature" could be more apt. It may be in their genes just as, in the opinion of many, homosexuality is. We all seek reciprocal love and if it is a fact that with some people, paedophilia is inborn and the striving for love can be satisfied only in this one strictly forbidden way, then, in those cases to which it applies, our loathing should be mixed with pity, though this, of course, does mot mean that we can ever allow them to act out their desires.

But surely, there is always self-satisfaction, often with the help of pornography? So a paedophile has this way out? No, not quite, for he can also be punished for obtaining or exchanging, on the internet for instance, pornographic material involving children, whereas we others may look at it, as long as it involves adults, to our heart's content as much and as often as we feel so inclined. More about this later.

If someone has sexual intercourse with a willing partner below the age of consent – i.e., with a person who is "technically" a child – he commits a punishable offence. But he cannot necessarily be classed as paedophile. He may in fact find the idea of paedophilia abhorrent and be not even aware of the fact that he has committed a crime; it often depends on the physical development and demeanour of the sexual partner.

This brings us to the next point: the age of the victim. It is often a small child, sexually as yet undeveloped and unable to defend itself against assault, persuasion or the exertion of authority. But a particularly young age is not necessarily a precondition. There are plenty of cases of 14-or 15-year-old boys being molested. It is the age *difference* between perpetrator and victim that plays a decisive part. This is the typical scenario between teacher and pupil, organist or priest and choirboy, family friend and young member of the family. This is what singles out the offence as so heinous and disgusting and makes it different from under-age sex between teenagers, although, let there be no doubt about it, rape or near-rape can be one of the features of that, too, as well as persuasion by unfair means. It seems, in the eyes of many teenagers, to be beginning to be almost shameful not to have "done it".

A paedophilic act need not necessarily mean physical involvement on the part of a child, let alone penetration. Exposing himself, masturbating in front of the child or inducing it to carry it out on the perpetrator may be sufficient. Actually, therefore, paedophilia, almost the worst sexual offence we know, can, contrary to most other such offences, be a sex crime with a minimum of, or no force, physical interference or compulsion being applied by the criminal. This may make a difference to the severity of punishment, but it is normally regarded as fully-fledged paedophilia all the same even where in strictly legal terms it is a lesser offence.

One of the main reasons for the violent dislike of this particular crime is that, whatever precise form it takes, it can damage – usually psychologically rather than physically – a child severely. I say "can", because, whilst this is often undoubtedly the case, it does not have to be so. Adults who have committed an offence, who are general failures or who sue for damages, are apt to put psychological damage in childhood forward in mitigation or it can be said to be the reason for a claim for substantial financial compensation, even if the event may have occurred 20 or more years ago and there can usually be no definite proof that the offence was committed at all and what effect it actually had on the child. Yet, if law reports in the papers are to be believed, the genuine or alleged victims are often given a large amount of credence. Many claims are undoubtedly true, but others are equally certain to be spurious if not entirely unfounded. But the accused is usually in a worse position from the outset, not to mention teachers who are in many cases suspended until the matter has been cleared up and who subsequently find it very difficult to live down the resulting gossip ("no smoke without fire").

The question is justified: are we certain that the trauma experienced is really always greater than, say, that of a child that happens to come across some sexual activity or even

221

intercourse between adults (not infrequently its own parents) and may have believed that one person was being violated by the other? The fact that most of us, at some time during our childhood encounter some sexual behaviour or acts that shock us does not mean that it has to affect us psychologically, let alone destroy us for the rest of our lives. If it were different, there would be very few sane and undamaged people about. And do not let us forget that plenty of people are disturbed or sexually perverted or inhibited, for quite different reasons and find a sexually traumatic offence against them, actual or invented, a convenient reason for their condition.

I am sure that quite a few children remain entirely unaffected. I remember an occasion when I came back to my parked car and found a gang of street urchins about to fill the motor with sand. When I threatened to call the police, one of them, by all appearances a perfectly normal child, asked me in all innocence, presumably in order to pacify me: "Shall I show you my dick?" For some children this sort of thing seems to be nothing particularly special and they are none the worse for it – which is certainly, let me say it once again, no excuse for committing paedophilia.[49]

And let us remember, too, that children, being naturally curious, often play "doctors" or "mummy and daddy" and are by no means as innocent as we like to think; or should I say, pretend? Sexual "education" of children is becoming more and more explicit. Hence I daresay that the effect of a paedophilic crime on these innocents may sometimes be exaggerated in the public mind. You can't have it both

---

[49] But if we are always so disgusted by paedophilia, why do we make it the subject of countless jokes playing it down? I cannot resist retelling one which I think significant however doubtful in taste. That of the six-year-old girl remarking to her friend "Mr. Smith on the second floor gives me 50p if I play with his penis." "What is a penis?" asks the other, mystified. "Same as a cock, only soft". Not much psychological damage there.

ways.[50]

Damage can also be done by children to one another. And there is no age limit. Theodore Dalrymple cites the case of a teacher who had to comfort a child of seven who had been horribly taunted and insulted by a class-mate. He had called him a "virgin".

Incidentally, let us not overlook how unreliable children can be as witnesses. During my practical legal training in Germany, I was, for a few months, attached to a criminal court specialising in sex crimes. As I seem to recall, children's testimony without additional proof was given more weight at that time in German than in British courts, and I was sometimes more than doubtful about some of the convictions on these occasions. The matter started typically with the mother noticing the genitals of her little boy being slightly inflamed, and "playing with oneself" being absolutely forbidden at the time took him severely to task. What easier excuse for the child than to allege that someone else, a grownup had done the "damage"? And I recall a case in which a labourer was accused of sexually molesting a five-year-old girl, a lovely little thing as innocent as a May morn. She described what he had done to her in the most realistic terms, without, incidentally, showing any trauma. This, in fact, was the accuser's salvation. In his cross-examination defending counsel was able to show that the whole thing had been an invention by the girl's mother who had resented the constant noise the accused had made with his saw and found the accusation the most convenient way of getting rid of him. She went to prison, but it had been a near thing to a perversion of justice. Personally I have shunned DIY ever since.

As I said in the beginning, you cannot punish anybody

---

[50] Vide this one: Sex lessons in an infant school. Any questions? One little girl raises her hand: "Can a girl of eight get a baby, Miss?" "No, Brenda, for a girl of eight this is quite impossible". At which a little boy, sitting behind her, bends forward and whispers audibly, "There you are, you windy little cow, what did I tell you!"

for their sexual tendencies, as long as they are not actively pursued. There are no doubt many latent, in the sense of inactive, homosexuals among us; why should this not be equally the case with paedophiles? And for that matter, most of us instinctively find small children cuddly and attractive. I happen to be one of them and have not infrequently been the object of somewhat suspicious glances by a mother if I happened to do as little as smile at her offspring whilst we were in a shop waiting to be served. It seems, again, that in this sphere it is always the worst that is suspected.

This can sometimes take on ludicrous forms. There was some time ago the case of a well-known married couple who had their holiday snaps developed in a chemist's shop and were reported to the police by an over-zealous shop assistant – for what? Some of the pictures showed their little girl – naked! The mind boggles. And take the recent case of an older woman seducing a 14- or 15-year-old boy. Yes, of course, it should not have happened, especially as she was, if I remember rightly, his teacher. But no matter. I am sure that, far from psychologically damaging the boy in question, she did him a favour. It was almost certainly a welcome and useful introduction into sex and probably of benefit to some of his future sex partners.

But why single out the public and the courts? Our authorities behave no differently. What is one to say about the directive by one local authority to all schools in its district that teachers should, on school excursions, have sunburn remedies handy so as to spray children protectively who had been unduly exposed to the sun. But only spraying! On no account must they rub it in – there was always the risk of it being classed as a sexual assault.[51] And what about the Home Secretary David Blunkett who considered lie detectors in order to make certain that convicted paedophiles had, after

---

[51] An interesting indication, incidentally, how our current compensation culture, or the fear of it, affects even the most innocent situations.

serving their sentence, shed their impure thoughts and had not been talking to children for any reason. If this rule were to be extended to its logical conclusion, bisexual rapists would obviously find it impossible to communicate with anybody at all and their only way out would be joining a Trappist monastery, if it would have them.

Let us go back for a moment to the risk of psychological damage to children caused by paedophiles. We are all sexual animals from our earliest childhood onwards. Originally we do not feel the need for restraint or shame. We have to be taught this for our own good and that of society. Is it so impossible that what we are trying so hard to teach our children does not always go all that deep and is not regarded by them in the same light as by us adults? Moreover, children like to be cuddled and being fussed over. Why should touching their most sensitive and pleasurable part – the sex organ – be so traumatic for them?[52] There – I knew it: You will say I am advocating it. Of course I am not – on the contrary. But the line between what is nice and what is traumatic is, in my view, very undefined.

Anyway, look at what happens a few years later: having been conditioned against sexual and semi-sexual contact, we then, at a certain age, have to unlearn all we have so laboriously acquired. Surprise, surprise, some things that were unconditionally taboo in our childhood, suddenly aren't bad after all; indeed they are indispensable for "good sex" and therefore encouraged. Very confusing as well as arbitrary.

What about the many "rings" disseminating paedophile literature? Basically I cannot see the difference between the effect of paedophilic and other pornographic literature. The allegation that pornography encourages bad sexual behaviour

[52] I remember a friend telling me laughingly about his 4-year-old daughter who liked to come into his bed in the morning, as children are apt to do. The first thing she used to do was to whip off her pyjama bottoms. (She grew up to be a very successful and balanced wife, mother and scientist).

or even violence, is unproven, however frequently it is put forward in mitigation by the defence counsel of a sex offender .On the contrary, pornography is often a desirable harmless outlet. This said, it is of course an inescapable fact that with paedophilic pornography, it is necessary to use children as models. This is, I agree, a decisive difference and for this reason producers and distributors do indeed deserve severe penalties. But here another question arises: Should consumers of this literature be punished as well, unless there are aggravating circumstances present? Before you say Yes, remember that today someone smoking marijuana is usually no longer punished, but the producer or supplier is. By the same token, it is largely forbidden to kill elephants for their tusks, but we don't punish a person who acquires an article made of ivory. The brothel keeper commits an offence, the customer goes scot-free. It is the supplier and not the consumer who is normally being punished. I am afraid I don't know the answer to this dilemma as far as child pornography is concerned, but it does make you think; after all, being a useful outlet for paedophiles, it could have the effect of reducing the actual crime. I am glad it is not me who has to weigh up the pros and cons.

To return to the question whether paedophiles are all the same and what to do about them. There are, of course, the worst kinds, the hardened criminals who habitually prey on children. They cannot be cured for the same reason for which homosexuals cannot be "cured": they like what they do; it is not an illness that can be treated. Castrating hardened paedophiles, which is sometimes suggested, would to my mind not be a viable option either, if only because it does not necessarily wipe out criminal sexual tendencies which might find expression in even worse crimes than sexual ones, if every way-out is blocked.

But for others it may have been a momentary aberration caused by the inability of expressing their sex life in the normal way. Some of them can possibly be treated and, if they wish to get rid of their affliction, should be given every chance to do so by affording them, regardless of cost, the best treatment medical science can devise; and I don't mean mere "counselling". I am certain this would do more towards reducing this kind of offence than long prison sentences, which after all are a financial burden on society, too. It is a question of whether we want retribution or a genuine reduction in the frequency of this crime, and the choice should be obvious.

What about the victims? As I already made clear, I do not believe in most cases in "lives having been destroyed" – these days, psychiatric treatment can overcome the trauma more often than not. I feel that such treatment preceded by an investigation whether it is necessary and has a chance of success should be automatic, if not compulsory for really affected victims at the state's expense if indeed the criminal cannot be made to pay for it. This would mitigate the consequences of the crime, and what could be more desirable?

Why is the public's attitude so hysterical? There could be many reasons. One is the behaviour of certain parts of the press. Theodore Dalrymple in his above-mentioned article ascribes it to the "confusion with regard to child and adult sexuality". I myself believe that the revulsion is on the one hand basically justified, but that it may often be greatly increased by our resistance against our own subconscious urges, deep down and suppressed, which we are most anxious to deny by expressing the utmost moral indignation. Whatever the reason, should there not be a more rational and enlightened investigation into causes, effects and the most successful prevention and mitigation?

That is all I wanted to show. You can condemn something without necessarily going over the top. Paedophilia seems a good example.

*